I0153250

# NORMAL CHRISTIAN

## GORDON MOORE

Ark House Press
arkhousepress.com

© 2023 Gordon J. Moore

All Scriptures are quoted from the New King James Version (NKJV) unless otherwise stated. © 1982 by Thomas Nelson. Used by permission. All rights reserved.

Scripture quotations marked AMP are taken from the Amplified Bible, © 2015 by The Lockman Foundation. Used by permission.

All rights reserved. No part of this publication may be reproduced, stored in a retrieval system or transmitted in any form or by any means electronic, mechanical, photocopying, recording or otherwise without the prior written permission of the publisher.

Cataloguing in Publication Data:
Title: Normal Christian
ISBN: 978-0-6458809-4-6 (pbk.)
Subjects: Leadership; Church;
Other Authors/Contributors: Moore, Gordon J

Published with Gordon J Moore
PO Box 46 Aspley Qld 4034 AUSTRALIA

# THE HOLY SCRIPTURES ARE OUR ETERNAL NORMAL

# Contents

# Introduction

*"I came that they may have life,*
*and may have it abundantly."*
*John 10:10 WEB*

One of my signature themes and messages for the last 50 years of ministry and leadership has centred on the good news of an abundant life in Christ.

Our Lord Jesus Christ came to set us free from sin and our old life, and give us a new one: eternal, empowered and abundant. This *"abundant life"* begins the moment we receive Jesus Christ as our Saviour and Lord.

We are born again supernaturally by the Holy Spirit and the Word of God!

*"Therefore, if anyone is in Christ,*
*he is a new creation:*
*old things have passed away;*
*behold, all things have become new."*
*2Corinthians 5:17*

The supernatural '*new birth*' provides us with a new life overflowing with God's favour, blessings and provisions - spiritually, emotionally, physically and materially.

This is the **FULL GOSPEL FOR THE WHOLE PERSON**!

> *"Beloved, I pray above all things that*
> *you may prosper and be in health,*
> *even as your soul prospers."*
> *3John 2*

So why the title of this book, "**NORMAL Christian**"? Is there such a thing as a '*normal Christian*'?

The starting point to answer such questions is to define '*normal*' from a Biblical point of view. For the Bible believing Christian **the Holy Scriptures are our ETERNAL NORMAL!**

## The Scriptures are the 'Rule of Faith' - THE ETERNAL NORMAL

From antiquity the early Christian leaders, such as Tertullian, used the term the '*Rule of Faith*' to describe the ultimate authority, or standard, of the Scriptures for all Christian belief, doctrine and living. The Word of God is the pattern, the blueprint and the standard for what a '*normal Christian life*' is.

There is to be no review, no reconsideration, no deconstruction and reconstruction, no reset, or no 'new normal'! The **ETERNAL NORMAL IS THE WORD OF GOD!**

## THE HOLY SCRIPTURES ARE OUR ETERNAL NORMAL!

The Scriptures provide us with the ruler, or yardstick, on which we are to base our lives and by which we measure and evaluate the genuineness of our faith and our progress in the Christian life.

The Scriptures explain exactly what the Lord Jesus Christ accomplished and provided for us on the cross through His death, burial and resurrection. These provisions are presented to us in the Bible in the form of promises.

*"By which have been given to us exceedingly*
*great and precious promises,*
*that through these you may be*
*partakers of the divine nature."*
*2Peter 1:4*

The big question is: Why is the provision of Christ in promise form?

The answer: **FAITH**

**The normal Christian life is a life of faith!**

The Christian life, therefore, is a life of faith in which the '*normal Christian*' lives in the provision of Christ as presented in the Bible, the Holy Scriptures.

> *"But without faith it is impossible to please Him:*
> *for he that comes to God must*
> *believe that He exists,*
> *and that He is a rewarder of them*
> *that diligently seek Him."*
> *Hebrews 11:6*

**The problem of settling for less than Christ's provision**

The biggest mistake we can make is to settle for less than what our heavenly Father has provided for us in Christ Jesus. If we accept any other standard apart from the Word of God we will find ourselves living far below that which has already been provided for us in Jesus Christ.

Instead of enjoying this abundant life in Christ, we may find ourselves living constantly restricted and bound by our needs, lacks, fears and problems.

## A life above and beyond our needs

God has provided for **ALL** His children to be living above and beyond their needs in every area of their lives; spiritually, mentally, emotionally, physically and materially. This 'abundant' provision in Jesus Christ is declared to us in His Word.

> *"I came that they may have and enjoy life,*
> *and have it in abundance [to*
> *the full, till it overflows]."*
> *John 10:10 Amplified Bible*

## Living by revelation

In order to experience this abundant life in Christ we need more than information, we need revelation concerning the truth of God's Word.

It is not discovered or uncovered by human intellect or effort, it is a gift from God through His Spirit.

*"But God has revealed them to us by His Spirit:*
*for the Spirit searches all things,*
*yes, the deep things of God.*
*For what man knows the things of a man,*
*except the spirit of man which is in him?*
*Even so no one knows the things of*
*God except the Spirit of God.*
*Now we have received, not the spirit of the*
*world, but the spirit who is from God,*
*that we might know the things that have*
*been freely given to us by God."*
*1Corinthians 2:10-12*

Once we have received this internal revelation of the Word of God from the Spirit of God we can live by faith.

We will then discover the experience and joy of living far above the limitations and restrictions of the circumstances, events, accusations and attitudes that the Devil uses to rob us, kill us and destroy our lives.

*"The thief does not come except to*
*steal, and to kill, and to destroy:*
*I am come that they might have life,*
*and that they might have it more abundantly."*
*John 10:10*

## An abundant life in Christ is God's normal

This book is written to declare to you the good news that it is totally '**NORMAL**', from God's point of view, for you and me to live an abundant life in Jesus Christ!

The purpose of this book is to present to you who you are, what you have and what you can do in Christ.

The Lord Jesus Christ has provided a life for us that is far bigger and better than we could ever imagine; an abundant life according to His rich supply above and beyond all our needs.

> *"But my God shall supply all your need according to his riches in glory by Christ Jesus."*
> *Philippians 4:19*

## The beyond life in Christ

This abundant life in Jesus Christ is a 'beyond life'; a life that is to be lived beyond ourselves, our limitations, our lacks, our doubts, our fears and our needs.

*"And God is able to make all
grace abound toward you;
that you, always having all
sufficiency in all things,
may abound to every good work."
2Corinthians 9:7*

This is just how the Lord Jesus Christ intended His Church to exist. Every believer living a '**normal Christian life**' - a favoured, blessed, bigger, beyond, prospered, abundant life!

**It is normal for the 'normal Christian'
to live a blessed, abundant, fruitful, victorious
and overflowing life in Christ Jesus!**

## Blessed to be a blessing

These blessings in Christ are so abundant that the '*normal Christian*' lives in overflow towards others; serving, giving, contributing and ministering for the encouragement, blessing, progress, building up and success of others!

*"From Whom all the body,
nourished and knit together by
joints and ligaments,*

*grows with the increase that is from God."*
*Colossians 2:19*

ENJOY!

Gordon Moore
AUTHOR

## Chapter One

# SPIRITUAL ORIGINS:
# "THE JUST SHALL LIVE BY FAITH"

To understand this blessed, abundant and full life that God has provided for all believers, we must first consider the foundation and the origins of this spiritual life.

**The normal Christian life is a life in the Holy Spirit**

**First, it is impossible to live the life of faith in Christ outside the supernatural empowerment of the Holy Spirit. Period!**

> *"Are you so foolish? Having begun in the Spirit, are you now being made perfect by the flesh?"*
> *Galatians 3:3*

The New Birth must be "**entered into supernaturally and be continued supernaturally, through the presence and power of the Holy Spirit**." *("Yes Holy Spirit", GJ Moore)*

## The two gifts of the new birth

The moment a person is born again two gifts are granted directly and instantly by the grace and power of God.

*"Jesus answered and said to him,*
*Most assuredly, I say to you,*
*unless one is born again,*
*he cannot* **SEE** *the kingdom of God.*
*Nicodemus said to Him, How can a*
*man be born when he is old?*
*Can he enter a second time into his*
*mother's womb and be born?*
*Jesus answered, Most assuredly, I say to you,*
*Unless one is born of water and the Spirit,*
*he cannot* **ENTER** *the kingdom of God.*
*That which is born of the flesh is flesh,*
*and* **that which is born of the Spirit is spirit**.*"*
*John 3:3-6*

## 1. The gift of REVELATION - to 'SEE'

This '**gift of revelation**' is the ability to "**see the kingdom**". This enables the believer to perceive, understand and know by revelation the spiritual truths and realities given by God.

> *"That the God of our Lord Jesus*
> *Christ, the Father of glory,*
> *may give to you **the spirit of wisdom and***
> ***revelation in the knowledge of Him***:
> *The eyes of your understanding*
> *being enlightened;*
> *that you might know what is*
> *the hope of His calling,*
> *and what the riches of the glory of*
> *His inheritance in the saints,*
> *And what is the exceeding greatness of*
> *His power toward us who believe,*
> *according to the working of His mighty power."*
> *Ephesians 1:17-19*

The gift of revelation is the foundation of Christian faith. This faith in Jesus Christ is based on revelation knowledge of God's Word revealed by the Holy Spirit.

*"Now we have received, not
the spirit of the world,
but the Spirit who is from God;
that we might know the things that have
been freely given to us of God.
These things we also speak, not in the
words which man's wisdom teaches,
but which the Holy Spirit teaches,
comparing spiritual things with spiritual."
1Cor 2:12-13*

## The born again child of God sees by revelation

*"He answered and said unto them,
Because it is given to you to know the
mysteries of the kingdom of heaven,
but to them it is not given.
But blessed are your eyes, for they see:
and your ears, for they hear."
Matt 13:11,16*

## 2. The gift of ENTRANCE - to 'EXPERIENCE'

This '**gift of entrance**' is the ability to "**enter the kingdom**". This enables the believer to actually know by personal experience the spiritual truths and realities given by God.

### The normal Christian lives by revelation and experience

> *"Jesus answered him, "I assure you*
> *and most solemnly say to you,*
> *unless a person is born again*
> *[reborn from above—*
> *spiritually transformed, renewed, sanctified],*
> *he cannot [ever] see and experience*
> *the kingdom of God."*
> *John 3:3 Amplified Bible*

It is this combination of **revelation** (spiritual insight and understanding) and **experience** (personal and practical entrance) that sets the believer in Christ apart and creates a truly spiritual person. This spiritual life in Christ is to be lived in and through the power of the Holy Spirit.

> *"That which is born of the Spirit is spirit."*
> *John 3:6*

## The normal Christian enters experience through revelation

Knowing the truth by revelation always proceeds knowing the truth by experience. It is the truth we know by revelation that sets us free! This is because we travel to what we see!

*"If you abide in My word, you*
*are My disciples indeed.*
*And you shall know the truth (revelation),*
*and the truth shall make you free (experience)."*
*John 8:31-32*

The apostles Paul and James both described this power to experience the life transforming power of truth as **"beholding in a mirror".** This "mirror" is the Word of God.

*"But we all, with unveiled face,*
***beholding as in a mirror the glory of the Lord,***
*are changed into the same*
*image from glory to glory,*
*even as by the Spirit of the Lord."*
*2Corinthians 3:18*

*"For if anyone is a hearer of the*
*word and not a doer,*
*he is like a man **observing his***

*natural face in a mirror;*
*For he observes himself, goes away, and*
*immediately forgets what kind of man he was.*
*But he who **looks into the perfect***
***law of liberty**, and continues in it,*
*and is not a forgetful hearer*
*but a doer of the work,*
*this one will be blessed in what he does."*
*James 1:23-25*

## Second, the just shall live by faith.

*"For therein is the righteousness of*
*God revealed from faith to faith:*
*as it is written, **The just shall live by faith**."*
*Romans 1:17*

The "*just*" are those who have been made right with God through their faith in Jesus Christ and are therefore "*spiritual*" by nature in the new creation.

*"But the natural man receives not*
*the things of the Spirit of God:*
*for they are foolishness to him:*
*neither can he know them,*
*because they are spiritually discerned."*

> *But he that is spiritual judges all things,*
> *yet he himself is judged of no man.*
> *For who has known the mind of the*
> *Lord, that he may instruct him?*
> *But we have the mind of Christ."*
> *1Corinthians 2:14-16*

The foundation of faith is the Word of God, but not just the 'written' Word of God by itself. True faith is also built on the 'revealed' Word of God.

'*Normal Christians*' do not read and know the Scriptures by information. Rather, they understand, comprehend and know the Scriptures by revelation and experience!

### It is normal for the spiritual person to know the truths of God's Word

The spiritual person, is not thinking and acting upon feelings, thoughts, philosophies, theology, circumstances, or what other people say, because that is mere information.

### Our calling is not to follow our hearts, our calling is to follow the Word of God that is planted in our hearts by the Holy Spirit

The spiritual person is believing, confessing, acting upon and living out from what has been revealed to him by the Holy Spirit in the Word of God.

> *"But as it is written, eye has*
> *not seen, nor ear heard,*
> *neither have entered into the heart of man,*
> *the things which God has prepared*
> *for them that love him.*
> *But God has **revealed them***
> ***to us by his Spirit..."***
> *1Corinthians 2:9-10*

Therefore, spiritual people are not looking **FOR** the victory, or **FOR** the freedom, or **FOR** the peace, or **FOR** the healing, or **FOR** the provision because they **ALREADY** possess those by faith!

Rather, the spiritual person is walking **IN** the victory, **IN** the freedom, **IN** the peace, **IN** the healing and **IN** the provision of Christ **BY FAITH**!

> *"No, in all these things we **ARE***
> *more than conquerors*
> *through Him who loved us."*
> *Romans 8:37*

This is because the 'normal Christian' **ALREADY POSSESSES** the promises of God by the revelation of faith; they have **ALREADY BEEN PROVIDED FOR** the believer **IN CHRIST**.

> *"What shall we then say to these things?*
> *If God be for us, who can be against us?*
> *He that spared not his own Son, but*
> *delivered him up for us all,*
> *how shall He not **with Him also***
> ***freely give us all things**?"*
> *Romans 8:31-32*

## The 'normal Christian' lives in the "*now*" of faith

The 'now *of faith*' is the time for the spiritual person.

Not the future, hoping God will act or do something sometime. Neither the past, resting in what God did do.

> *"**Now faith is**…"*
> *Hebrews 11:1*

The spiritual person's faith is active in the **'NOW';** living and moving in faith in the present in obedience to the Holy Spirit's leading.

## The spiritual person is focused on obeying the leading of the Holy Spirit in the NOW, in the PRESENT, in the MOMENT!

The spiritual person is not waiting for God to provide. He is accepting by faith in the "*now*" that Christ has already provided according to His Word!

## The Normal Christian lives in the PRESENT and CONTINUOUS FACT of the FULL, COMPLETE, SUFFICIENT and FINISHED work of Christ!

Therefore, the 'normal Christian' thinks, speaks and acts according to the fact of Christ's accomplished provision! Their focus, trust and reliance is upon what the Word of God declares, not on what the natural is presenting.

**"The Spiritual Man does not rely on, or live by his feelings or thoughts- his feelings and thoughts tell him nothing, unless they agree with the Word of God!" (H Greenwood)**

**Faith is the spiritual person's substance, assurance, evidence and comprehension.**

*"**Now faith is** the **substance**
of things hoped for,
the **evidence** of things not seen."
Hebrews 11:1*

*"Now faith is the **assurance**
(title deed, confirmation)
of things hoped for (divinely guaranteed),
and the **evidence** of things not seen
[the conviction of their reality—
faith **comprehends** as fact what cannot be
experienced by the physical senses]."
Hebrews 11:1 Amplified Bible*

## Living for the approval of God

Living by revelation is a life of obedience in faith. It is simply living by faith from what God has revealed and is revealing in His Word, the Bible, and by the Holy Spirit.

The life of faith is never concerned about following man-made rules, laws, requirements or expectations.

The primary focus of the '*normal Christian*' is to obey and please Christ by faith. This is an internal life in the Spirit, receiving praise and approval from God.

*"But he is a Jew, who is one inwardly;*
*and circumcision is of the heart, in*
*the spirit, and not in the letter;*
*whose praise is not of men, but of God."*
*Romans 2:29*

## Living from the 'inside-out', internal in the Spirit

This life of revelation is internal in the spirit, not external in the physical. Therefore, a '*normal Christian life*' is lived from the 'inside-out', that is, from the spiritual to the physical, rather than from the 'outside-in', or from the physical to the spiritual.

The spiritual person is not living by the 5 senses 'outwardly in the flesh', but rather, 'inwardly by faith in the Spirit'; by what God says in His Word and reveals by the Holy Spirit.

Therefore, 'revelation faith' is constantly looking at the "*unseen in the spirit*", or the spiritual realities and truths revealed in the Word of God. This is the '*normal Christian life*'.

*"While we look not at the things which are seen,*
*but at the things which are not seen:*
*for the things which are seen are temporal;*
*but the things which are not seen are eternal."*
*2Corinthians 4:18*

## Walking through the valleys

The spiritual person experiences the 'valleys of life' just like any other person. And like David the Psalmist, they keep walking in faith "**through**" their circumstances.

This is because the spiritual person knows that God is with them even in the valleys! Therefore, there is no room for the fear of evil in the heart of faith of the spiritual person!

> *"Yes, though I **walk through** the*
> *valley of the shadow of death,*
> *I will fear no evil, for **You are with me**,*
> *Your **rod** and **staff** they comfort me."*
> *Psalm 23:4*

## Correction and protection in the valleys

The spiritual person realises that 'valley experiences' of life (difficulties, challenges and problems) can be beneficial for them because of the provision of God's "*rod*" and "*staff*".

The "*rod*" is God's **loving correction,** which causes the spiritual person to make adjustments and change as they are **guided** by the Spirit through the valleys of life.

The "**staff**" is God's **loving protection** which keeps the spiritual person from evil as they are **guarded** by the Spirit through the valleys of life.

Therefore, good comes out of every experience. This is the 'normal Christian' perspective!

The perspective of the spiritual person is different because of the faith that understands God will even turn bad things out for good!

> *"And we know that all things work together*
> *for good to those who love God,*
> *and are the called according to His purpose."*
> *Romans 8:28*

And so, even in times of trials and difficulties the spiritual person is not destroyed, hindered or bewildered by what is happening in the physical, or in the circumstances surrounding them. They are motivated and strengthened from within by the presence, power and leading of the Holy Spirit.

## Living in the Fulness of Christ

As a result of living by the revelation of faith in the promises of God, the '*normal Christian*' is "*partaking of the divine nature*" of God and lives in God's abundant provision in Christ in every area of life.

> *"Whereby are given to us exceeding*
> *great and precious promises:*
> *that by these you might be*
> *partakers of the divine nature,*
> *having escaped the corruption that*
> *is in the world through lust."*
> *2Peter 1:4*

This is living in the "*fulness of Christ*".

> *"For out of His fullness [the superabundance*
> *of His grace and truth]*
> *we have all received grace upon grace*
> *[spiritual blessing upon spiritual blessing,*
> *favour upon favour, and gift heaped upon gift]."*
> *John 1:16 Amplified Bible*

The apostle Paul prayed that every believer would possess this revelation so that they would live far above and beyond mere human knowledge and understanding. This would result in them being "*filled with all the fulness of God*" through the power of the Holy Spirit.

*"And to know the love of Christ,*
*which passes knowledge,*
*that you might be filled with*
*all the fulness of God.*
*Now to Him who is able to do exceeding*
*abundantly above all that we ask or think,*
*according to the power that works in us."*
*Ephesians 3:19-20*

The Amplified Bible is helpful in clarifying the meaning of this verse.

*"...that you may be*
*filled up [throughout your being]*
*to all the fullness of God*
*[so that you may have*
*the richest experience of God's*
*presence in your lives,*
*completely filled and flooded*
*with God Himself]."*
*Ephesians 3:19-20 Amplified Bible*

## IT IS NORMAL FOR THE SPIRITUAL PERSON TO LIVE IN THE FULLNESS OF GOD IN CHRIST!

## Chapter Two

# "THE SPIRITUAL PERSON"

*"That the righteousness of the*
*law might be fulfilled in us,*
*who walk not after the flesh, but after the Spirit.*
*For they that are after the flesh do*
*mind the things of the flesh;*
*but they that are after the Spirit*
*the things of the Spirit.*
*For to be carnally minded is death;*
*but to be spiritually minded is life and peace."*
*Romans 8:4-6*

### Paul's three men

In his epistles the apostle Paul uses three men to illustrate
the three positions that we can find ourselves in spiritually;

the "*Natural Man*" (1Cor 2:14), the "*Carnal Man*" (Rom 7:14) and the "*Spiritual Man*" (1Cor 2:15)

## The Natural Man

The first, the "**Natural Man**", *from "psuchikos" (Strongs Concordance, G5591),* means *"governed by breath, the sensuous nature with it's subjection to appetite and passion".*

*The "natural man"* is the unregenerate, non-spiritual and sensuous person who is subject to their natural appetites and passions and is living by the 5 senses.

The *"natural man"* might be intelligent, eloquent and educated but spiritual insight into the Scriptures and the things of God are totally hidden from him, in fact, *"they are foolishness to him".*

> *"But the natural man does not receive*
> *the things of the Spirit of God:*
> *for they are foolishness to him:*
> *neither can he know them,*
> *because they are spiritually discerned.*
> *1Corinthians 2:14*

## The Spiritual Man

The second, the "**Spiritual Man**", is from the Greek word "*pneumatikos*" (Strongs Concordance, G4152) which means, "*belonging to the divine spirit, of God the Holy Spirit, one who is filled with and governed by the spirit of God*"

The "*Spiritual Man*" is the born again, renewed, Spirit indwelt, Spirit filled, Spirit empowered, Spirit led and Spirit governed person.

> *"But you are not in the flesh but in the Spirit,*
> *if indeed the Spirit of God dwells in you.*
> *Now if anyone does not have the*
> *Spirit of Christ, he is not His."*
> *Romans 8:9*

## The 'spiritual man' lives contrary to the 'natural man'

The "*natural man*" is the direct opposite of the "*spiritual man*". This is because spiritual people are enlightened, empowered and directed by the Holy Spirit. Therefore, they think, speak and act contrary to the natural person who is influenced and guided by the "*spirit of the world*" through the 5 senses.

> *"Now we have received, not*
> *the spirit of the world,*
> *but the Spirit who is from God;*
> *that we might know the things that*
> *are freely given to us by God."*
> *1Corinthians 2:12*

## The Carnal Man

The third, the '**carnal man**', from *"sarkikos"* (Strongs Concordance, G4559) means *"having the nature of flesh, under the control of the animal appetites and the concept of depravity"*.

*The 'carnal man'* is the regenerated Christian who, because of his own choices and disobedience, is controlled by natural appetites and passions rather than by the Spirit of God.

Therefore, this *'carnally minded Christian'* finds himself living a life of defeat and condemnation out of which he exclaims, *"O wretched man that I am!"* (Romans 7:24)

The problem for the *'carnal man'* is that he does not live by the power of the Holy Spirit in the new creation and so finds himself constantly defeated and 'stuck' in Romans chapter 7!

Although he knows what is right and he wants to do what is right, he is powerless to do so!

> *"For we know that the law is spiritual:*
> *but I am carnal, sold under sin.*
> *For that which I do I allow not: for*
> *what I would, that do I not;*
> *but what I hate, that do I."*
> *Romans 7:14-15*

## Overview of Paul's 3 Men

Paul's 3 men are outlined in 1Corinthians 2:1-3:8, Romans 7:1-25, Romans 8:1-39 and Hebrews 5:12-14, 6:1-3.

The following chart summarises and compares the characteristics of each man or spiritual state in which we live.

| NATURAL MAN | CARNAL MAN | SPIRITUAL MAN |
|---|---|---|
| Ignorance | Confusion | Revelation Knowledge |
| Self minded | Fleshly minded | Spiritually minded |
| Blind | Short-sighted | Full Sight |

| Lawless | Unlawful | Law fulfilling |
| Foolish | Unwise | Wise |
| Darkness | Shadows | Light |
| Ruled by 5 senses | 5 Senses/Spirit mixture | Word and Spirit |
| Sinner | Sinful | Saint |
| Bondage | Struggle | Freedom |
| Impotent | Powerless | Powerful |
| Barren | Unfruitful | Fruitful |
| Empty | Blockages | Overflow |
| Unborn | Babe/Immature | Mature |
| Wayside ground | Stony/Thorny ground | Good Ground ("*30/60/100 fold*") |

## The spiritual person lives in Romans chapter 8!

The supernatural and life transforming experience of Romans chapter 6, which describes the new birth experience, propels the newly created spiritual person into Romans chapter 8.

And so, when reading Romans chapter 6 and chapter 8 together we discover that the language and attitude in both chapters of empowerment and victory over sin, the flesh and the devil is consistent.

*"Therefore we are buried with
him by baptism into death:
that like as Christ was raised up from
the dead by the glory of the Father,
even so we also should walk in newness of life.
For if we have been planted together
in the likeness of his death,
we shall be also in the likeness
of his resurrection."
Romans 6:4-5*

*"There is therefore now no condemnation
to them which are in Christ Jesus,
who walk not after the flesh, but after the Spirit.
For the law of the Spirit of life in Christ Jesus
has made me free from the
law of sin and death."
Romans 8:1-2*

This is contrary to chapter 7, which describes the plight of a 'carnal Christian' labouring under the power of sin. The apostle Paul uses himself as an example, "*I am carnal*", to show the intense struggle and the personal sense of overwhelming defeat and condemnation felt by the carnal Christian.

*"I am carnal, sold under sin."
Romans 7:14*

Furthermore, the apostle Paul uses himself to demonstrate that even though he is an apostle, he too can slip back into this carnal state of being overpowered by sin through disobedience.

## The secret: Personal discipline

> *"But I discipline my body and*
> *bring it into subjection,*
> *lest, when I have preached to others,*
> *I myself should become disqualified."*
> *1Corinthians 9:27*

## One step away from reversion to our carnal self

The problem we all face, because we live in the natural world, is that we are all susceptible to temptation and acts of disobedience, which will cause us to revert to our carnal self.

This is why the apostle Paul repeatedly exhorts us through his epistles to remain constantly vigilant and not ignorant of the devil's devices.

> *"Now all these things happened*
> *unto them for examples,*

*and they are written for our admonition, upon*
*whom the ends of the world are come.*
**Therefore, let him who thinks he**
**stands take heed lest he fall.**
*There has no temptation taken you*
*but such as is common to man:*
*but God is faithful, who will not suffer you*
*to be tempted above that ye are able;*
*but will with the temptation also*
*make a way to escape,*
*that ye may be able to bear it."*
*1Cor 10:11-13*

## The spiritual person finds it 'more normal' to live righteously

However, the more a spiritual person lives in the Holy Spirit and discovers the power of being *"spiritually minded"*, he finds that it is 'more normal' not to sin!

This is because the spiritual person carries *"God's seed"*, or nature and character, within him and is empowered to continually make right choices on a daily basis.

This builds a resilience and resistance within the spiritual person's life which builds '**habitual righteousness**', rather than building '**habitual sin**'.

*"No one born (begotten) of God*
*[deliberately, knowingly, and*
*habitually] practices sin,*
*for God's nature abides in him*
*[His principle of life,*
*the divine sperm, remains*
*permanently within him];*
*and he cannot practice sinning because*
*he is born (begotten) of God."*
*1John 3:9 Amplified Bible*

The carnal Christian does not have to stay in his defeated and confused state. Rather, he can discover once again the victory and power over sin through the **always available provision of Christ**!

It is through faith in the Lord Jesus Christ that we are delivered from sin and our carnal self!

*"O wretched man that I am!*
*who shall deliver me from the*
*body of this death?*
**I thank God through Jesus Christ our Lord!***"*
*Romans 6:24-25*

## Taking up the cross daily

This victory over sin, as outlined in Romans chapter 6, is discovered through making the daily, conscious and habitual decision of "*taking up our cross and following Christ*".

> "*And he said to them all, If any man will come after me, let him deny himself, and **take up his cross daily**, and follow me.*"
> *Luke 9:23*

It is by taking up our cross daily by faith, that we "*reckon*", or "*consider*" (Amplified Bible), ourselves to be "*dead indeed to sin, but alive to God*"!

> "*For the that He died, He died for sin once for all; but the life that He lives, He lives to God. Likewise you also, reckon yourselves to be dead indeed to sin, but alive to God in Jesus Christ our Lord.*"
> *Romans 6:10-11*

To the spiritual person it is a simple matter of deciding to stop sinning because this is what God wants!

The secret to living in victory over our carnal, sinful self, or our old nature, is to live by faith in Christ's provision through His cross in Romans chapter 6. This is how we "**die to sin**" and "**live to God**" by faith in Christ in Romans chapter 8!

*"But you are not in the flesh but in the Spirit,*
*if indeed the Spirit of God dwells in you.*
*Now if anyone does not have the*
*Spirit of Christ, he is not His.*
*And if Christ is in you, the body*
*is dead because of sin;*
*but the Spirit is life because of righteousness."*
*Romans 8:9-10*

## 'Disciples' not just 'believers'

The death, burial and resurrection of Jesus Christ is the complete and perfect provision for our sins and for our new life in Christ. However, this provision of Christ must be appropriated by faith for it to be effective in our lives.

It is in the daily and habitual appropriation of Christ's provision through the obedience of faith that we are approved by God.

## Transformed into Christ - from *"believer"* to *"disciple"*

This transforms the *'believer'* into a *'disciple'* of Jesus Christ. They are no longer just a *'believer'*, but have been transformed experientially and practically by their belief.

This makes the difference between a *'Christian'* (one who believes **IN** Christ) and a *'Disciple'* (one who has been transformed **INTO** Christ)!

The apostle Luke identifies this difference and progression of faith when he first called the new members of the church *"believers"* in Acts 2:43, and then calls them *"disciples"* in Acts 6:1.

What changed for Luke to identify them differently? It was the progression from a person who had experienced salvation and *"believed"* in Christ, to a *"disciple"* who had progressed through **obeying** Christ in his practical, daily life.

The first believers committed themselves to the apostle's doctrine and teaching, prayer and praise, fellowship with the church community, hospitality in homes, meeting each other's needs and evangelising the unchurched.

It is through the daily participation in these activities that they progressed from mere belief in Christ to actively living in Christ!

> *"And they continued steadfastly in the*
> *apostles' doctrine and fellowship,*
> *and in breaking of bread, and in prayers.*
> *And all who **believed** were together,*
> *and had all things common;*
> *And sold their possessions and goods,*
> *and parted them to all men,*
> *as every man had need.*
> *And they, continuing daily with*
> *one accord in the temple,*
> *and breaking bread from house to house,*
> *did eat their food with gladness*
> *and singleness of heart,*
> *Praising God, and having favour*
> *with all the people.*
> *And the Lord added to the church daily*
> *those who were being saved."*
> *Acts 2:41-47*

> *"And the word of God increased;*
> *and the number of the **disciples***
> *multiplied in Jerusalem greatly;*

> *and a great company of the priests*
> *were obedient to the faith."*
> *Acts 6:7*

**Dealing with sin, not just sins**

The choice of words in the Scriptures are important to note.

For example, from Romans chapter 1 through to the first half of chapter 5, the apostle Paul uses the word "***sins***" (plural).

Half way through Romans chapter 5 through to chapter 6 he changes and uses the word "***sin***" (singular). Why is this?

The apostle Paul is showing us that there are two aspects of the work of sin in our lives.

First, "***sins***", refers to the sins that we personally commit or practice (what we do), and second, "***sin***" refers to us as a "***sinner***" because of our inherent "***sinful nature***" (who we are).

> *"So now [if that is the case, then]*
> *it is no longer I who do it*
> *[the disobedient thing which I despise],*
> *but the **sin [nature]** which lives in me.*
> *1 Corinthians 3:1 (AMP)*

*"We know that our **old self** [our human
nature without the Holy Spirit]
was nailed to the cross with Him,
in order that our **body of sin**
might be done away with,
so that we would no longer be slaves to sin."
Romans 6:6 Amplified Bible*

## The cross of Christ deals with both aspects of sin

First, Jesus Christ died on the cross to pay the penalty for
our **"sins"** as the lamb of God, our **Saviour**.

*"Who his own self bore our sins in
His own body on the tree,
that we, being dead to sins, should
live to righteousness:
by whose stripes you were healed."
1Peter 2:24*

We are forgiven of our "**sins"**, what we have done, and
the penalty of death is removed (Romans 3:23). We are
justified and made right before God!

*"Therefore being justified by faith,
we have peace with God through
our Lord Jesus Christ:*

*By whom also we have access by faith
into this grace wherein we stand,
and rejoice in hope of the glory of God."
Romans 5:1-2*

Second, Jesus Christ rose again to conquer and remove the **power of "sin"** in our human nature as our risen, conquering Lord!

Jesus Christ destroys our "**body of sin**", our sinful nature, making our "*old man*" obsolete and powerless through our faith in Him.

*"Knowing this, that our old man
is crucified with Him,
that the **body of sin** might be destroyed,
that henceforth we should not serve **sin**.
For he that is dead is **freed from sin**."
Romans 6:6-7*

## Servants of God and righteousness

We are now set free from the power of sin in order that we might live sanctified and holy lives as "slaves (*servants) of God*" (Romans 6:22).

*"And having been set free from sin,*
*you became **slaves of righteousness**.*

*But now having been set free from sin*
*and having become **slaves of God**,*
*you have your fruit to holiness,*
*and the end everlasting life."*
*Romans 6:18, 22*

In Christ, we have been transformed and made the "**righteousness of God in Christ Jesus**"! This is why it is more normal for the spiritual person to serve righteousness rather than sin. This is not because he is trying to do righteous things, it is because he **IS** "*the righteousness of God*"!

*"For He has made Him to be sin*
*for us, who knew no sin;*
*that we might be made the*
*righteousness of God in Him."*
*2Corinthians 5:21*

## Dead, buried and raised with Christ

The spiritual person identifies fully with the death, burial and resurrection of Christ by faith. This propels them into "*newness life*" by the resurrection power of the Lord Jesus Christ!

> *"Therefore we are buried with*
> *him by baptism into death:*
> *that like as Christ was raised up from*
> *the dead by the glory of the Father,*
> *even so we also should walk in newness of life.*
> *For if we have been planted together*
> *in the likeness of his death,*
> *we shall be also in the likeness*
> *of his resurrection."*
> *Romans 6:4*

## The Two World Orders - the Flesh and the Spirit

The environment in which we all live is divided into the 'two world orders' of the "**flesh**" and the "**Spirit**".

> *"There is therefore now no condemnation*
> *to those who are in Christ Jesus,*
> *who do not walk according the **flesh**,*
> *but according the **Spirit**."*
> *Romans 8:1*

The apostle Paul elaborates on the nature of these two world orders as being either "**carnally minded**" or "**spiritually minded**" (Romans 8:7).

These orders are diametrically opposed to each other because the first, the order of the flesh, operates on the principle of "*death*" and the second, the order of the Spirit, operates on the principle of "*life and peace*".

The order of the flesh is an enemy of God, because it is "*not subject to the law of God*".

> *"For to be **carnally minded** is **death**,*
> *but to be **spiritually minded** is **life and peace**.*
> *Because the carnal mind is enmity against God;*
> *for it is not subject to the law of*
> *God, nor indeed can be.*
> *So then, those who are in the*
> *flesh cannot please God.*
> *But you are not in the flesh but in the Spirit,*
> *if indeed the Spirit of God dwell in you."*
> *Romans 8:7-9*

The Scriptures also define these two orders as "**the world**" and "**the kingdom**".

> *"Jesus answered, **My kingdom**
> is not of **this world**:
> if my kingdom were of this world,
> then would my servants fight,
> that I should not be delivered to the Jews:
> but now is my kingdom not from here."*
> *John 18:36*

## The Order of "the world"

The Greek word for "**world**" is "*cosmos*" (Strongs Concordance, G2889) meaning "*the arrangement and order of things*", or the 'moral world'. The apostle John declared that this "*world*" was under the power of the devil and opposing God.

> *"We know [for a fact] that we are of God,
> and **the whole world [around us]
> lies in the power of the evil one**
> [opposing God and His precepts]."*
> *1John 5:19 Amplified Bible*

The order of the world is comprised of:-

* "the "**WORLD**" - "*lust of the flesh*", "*lust of the eyes*" and "*the pride of life*"

* the "**FLESH**" - the '5 senses' contained in the "*body of sin*" and the "*body of death*"
* the "**DEVIL**" - Satan, the evil father of lies, rebellion and sin

*"Love not the world, neither the*
*things that are in the world.*
*If any man love the world, the love*
*of the Father is not in him.*
*For all that is in the world, the lust of*
*the flesh, and the lust of the eyes,*
*and the pride of life, is not of the*
*Father, but is of the world.*
*And the world passes away, and the lust thereof:*
*but he that does the will of*
*God abides for ever."*
*1John 2:15-17*

## The Order of "the Kingdom"

The Greek word for "**kingdom**" is "*basileia*" (Strongs Concordance, G932) meaning "*royal power, kingship, dominion and rule*", or the royal power of Jesus Christ the Lord.

*"He has delivered us from the*
*power of darkness,*

> *and conveyed us into the kingdom*
> *of the Son of His love."*
> *Colossians 1:13*

The order of the kingdom is comprised of a three fold witness:-

- \* "the "**WATER**"
- \* the "**BLOOD**"
- \* the "**SPIRIT**"

> *"And there are three that bear witness in earth,*
> *the **spirit**, and the **water**, and the **blood**:*
> *and these three agree in one.*
> *If we receive the witness of men,*
> *the witness of God is greater:*
> *for this is the witness of God which*
> *He has testified of His Son."*
> *1John 5:8-9*

## The witness of God in Christ

The Lord Jesus Christ came to establish the witness, or testimony, of God and His kingdom to the world through each of these:-

\*    "the "**WATER**" - the word of the Father at the baptism of Jesus Christ

*"When He had been baptised,*
*Jesus came up immediately from the water;*
*and behold, the heavens were opened to Him,*
*and He saw the Spirit of God descending*
*like a dove, and alighting upon Him.*
*And suddenly a voice came from heaven, saying,*
*This is my beloved Son, in whom*
*I am well pleased."*
*Matthew 3:16-17*

\*    the "**BLOOD**" - the events, accomplishments and provisions of the death, burial and resurrection of Jesus Christ

*"But one of the soldiers pierced*
*his side with a spear,*
*and immediately blood and water came out.*
*And he who has seen has testified,*
*and his testimony is true;*
*and he knows that he is telling the*
*truth, so that you may believe."*
*John 19:34-3*

*"to Jesus the Mediator of the new
covenant, and to the blood of sprinkling
that speaks better things than that of Abel."
Hebrews 12:24*

\*   the "**SPIRIT**" - the empowering and life-giving
Spirit of God without measure in Christ

*"He must increase, but I must decrease.
He who comes from above is above all;
he who is of the earth is earthly,
and speaks of the earth:
He who comes from heaven is above all.
And what He has seen and
heard, that he testifies;
and no one receives His testimony.
He who has received His testimony
has certified that God is true.
For He whom God has sent
speaks the words of God,*
**for God does not give the Spirit by measure.**
*The Father loves the Son, and has
given all things into His hand."
John 3:30-35*

*"This is He that came by **water and blood**, even Jesus Christ;*
*not by water only, but by water and blood.*
*And it is **the Spirit that bears witness**,*
*because the Spirit is truth."*
*1John 5:6*

## The witness of Christ in the normal Christian

The 'normal Christian' has this same threefold testimony, or witness, of Christ within him:-

*"**He who believes in the Son of God has the witness in himself;***
*he who does not believe God*
*has made Him a liar;*
*because he has not believed the testimony*
*that God has given of his Son.*
*And this is the testimony;*
*that God has given us eternal life,*
*and this life is in his Son.*
*He who has the Son has life;*
*he who does not have the Son*
*of God does not have life."*
*1John 5:10-12*

\*    "the "**WATER**" - regeneration and new birth by the washing of the Word of God

> *"Having been born again, not of*
> *corruptible seed, but of incorruptible,*
> *by the word of God, which lives*
> *and abides for ever."*
> *1Peter 1:23*

> *"Not by works of righteousness*
> *which we have done,*
> *but according to His mercy He has saved us,*
> *by the washing of regeneration, and*
> *renewing of the Holy Spirit."*
> *Titus 3:5*

\*    the "**BLOOD**" - "the complete and perfect provisions, victory and new life of the cross of Jesus Christ

> *"Knowing that you were not redeemed*
> *with corruptible things,*
> *like silver and gold, from your aimless conduct*
> *received by tradition from your fathers,*
> *but with the precious blood of Christ,*
> *as of a lamb without blemish and without spot."*
> *1Peter 1:18-19*

\*     the "**SPIRIT**" - the empowered, victorious and abundant Spirit filled life

*"That which is born of the flesh is flesh;*
*and that which is born of the Spirit is spirit."*
*John 3:6*

## Chapter Three

# THE MINDSET OF THE SPIRITUAL PERSON

*"Now we have received, not the spirit of
the world, but the spirit which is of God;
that we might know the things that
are freely given to us of God.
Which things also we speak, not in the
words which man's wisdom teaches,
but which the Holy Spirit teaches;
comparing spiritual things with spiritual.
But the natural man does not receive
the things of the Spirit of God:
for they are foolishness to him:
neither can he know them,
because they are spiritually discerned.
But he that is spiritual judges all things,
yet he himself is judged by no man.*

> *For who has known the mind of the*
> *Lord, that he may instruct him?*
> *But we have the mind of Christ."*
> *1Corinthians 2:12-16*

The normal Christian has been renewed in his mind through the new birth. This has completely transformed his thinking, giving him a new mindset about everything.

It is therefore normal for a spiritual person to see things from God's viewpoint.

> *"And do not be conformed to this world,*
> *but be transformed by the*
> *renewing of your mind,*
> *that you may prove what is that good and*
> *acceptable and perfect will of God."*
> *Romans 12:2*

The spiritual person has only one confidence and that is in Christ alone!

For the '*normal Christian*' confidence in the flesh, or the natural mind, is a dangerous concept because the flesh is unstable like shifting sand and is contrary to the ways of God.

*"for we [who are born-again have
been reborn from above—
spiritually transformed, renewed,
set apart for His purpose and]
are the true circumcision, who worship
in the Spirit of God and glory
**and take pride and exult in Christ Jesus
and place no confidence
[in what we have or who we are] in the flesh."***
*Philippians 3:3 Amplified Bible*

## The spiritual person is *"judging all things"*

A spiritual person perceives and looks at life from God's perspective, they see everything from God's view of things. This is because they have been granted spiritual sight, discernment and understanding.

*"But the spiritual man [the spiritually
mature Christian] **judges all things
[questions, examines and applies
what the Holy Spirit reveals],***
*yet is himself judged by no one
[the unbeliever cannot judge and understand
the believer's spiritual nature].
For WHO HAS KNOWN THE MIND*

> *and PURPOSES OF THE LORD,*
> *SO AS TO INSTRUCT HIM?*
> **But we have the mind of Christ**
> **[to be guided by His thoughts and purposes]**.
> *1Corinthians 2:15-16 Amplified Bible*

## Judging all things

The spiritual person, therefore, is constantly "**questioning, examining and applying what the Holy Spirit reveals"** (Amplified Bible).

Everything is measured, evaluated and "*judged"* by what God says in His Word and reveals by the Holy Spirit!

## Judging to identify and qualify what is righteous

This kind of judgement by the spiritual person is not a negative one in the sense of disqualification or criticism, or even because of a fear of doing wrong.

Rather, it is a judgement to identify and qualify what is righteous, good and virtuous and therefore, pleasing to God.

> *"Finally, brethren, whatever things are*
> *true, whatever things are noble,*
> *whatever things are just,*

> *whatever things are pure,*
> *whatever things are lovely, whatever*
> *things are of good report;*
> *if there is any virtue, if there is*
> *anything praiseworthy-*
> *meditate on these things."*
> *Philippians 4:8*

The Scriptures teach us to *"test all things carefully"* so that we will be able to identify, hold on to and practice what is good and pleasing to God.

> *"But test all things carefully [so you*
> *can recognise what is good].*
> *Hold firmly to that which is good."*
> *1 Thessalonians 5:21 Amplified Bible*

## "Judge not lest you be judged"

A most commonly misunderstood, misused and misquoted Scripture, by Christians and the non-Christians alike, is Jesus' teaching on judgement in the gospel of Matthew.

> *"Judge not, that you be not judged.*
> *For with what judgment you*
> *judge, you will be judged;*

*and with the measure you use, it
will be measured back to you.
And why do you look at the speck
in your brother's eye,
but do not consider the plank in your own eye?
Or how can you say to your brother, 'Let
me remove the speck from your eye';
and, look, a plank is in your own eye?
Hypocrite, **first** remove the
plank from your own eye
and **then** you will see clearly to remove
the speck from your brother's eye."
Matthew 7:1-5*

## Self judgement first

However Jesus' point was not about not judging others, but rather about **judging ourselves first** before we judge others!

*"**Examine yourselves** as to
whether you are in the faith.
**Test yourselves**.
Do you not know yourselves,
that Jesus Christ is in you?
- unless indeed you are disqualified.*

> *But I trust that you will know that*
> *we are not disqualified."*
> *2Corinthians 13:5-6*

Furthermore, when it is necessary to judge others we ought do it justly without severity and in grace, as we will be judged with *"the same measure we use"*!

## The hypocrisy of the pharisees

Jesus was speaking directly to the hypocrisy of the pharisees who were quick to judge others, yet they were guilty of the same and even worse sins! They were keen to teach others but failed to teach themselves first!

> *"Indeed you are called a Jew, and rest*
> *the law, and make your boast in God,*
> *And know His will, and approve*
> *the things that are excellent,*
> *being instructed out of the law,*
> *And are confident that you yourself*
> *are a guide of the blind,*
> *a light of them who are in darkness,*
> *an instructor of the foolish, a teacher of babes,*
> *having the form of knowledge*
> *and truth in the law.*

*You, therefore, who teach another,*
*you teach yourself?*
*You who preach that a man should*
*not steal, do you steal?*
*You who say, "do not commit adultery",*
*do you commit adultery?*
*You who abhor idols, do you rob rob temples?*
*You who make your boast of the law,*
*do you dishonour God through*
*breaking the law?*
*For the name of God is blasphemed among*
*the Gentiles through you, as it is written."*
*Romans 2:17-24*

## Judging all things is normal for a spiritual person

It is normal, therefore, for a spiritual person to judge, test, examine, qualify and prove all things, starting with himself first!

*"But let each one **examine his own work**,*
*and then he will have rejoicing in*
*himself alone, and not in another. "*
*Galatians 6:4*

**Self examination and judgement leads to clearer sight and a better understanding of self and others**

> *"Hypocrite, **first** remove the*
> *plank from your own eye*
> *and **then you will see clearly** to remove*
> *the speck from your brother's eye."*
> *Matthew 7:5*

**Self examination and judgement leads to spiritual and physical health**

> *"But let a man **examine himself**,*
> *and so let him eat of the bread,*
> *and drink of the cup.*
> *For he who eats and drinks in*
> *an unworthy manner,*
> *eats and drinks judgement to himself,*
> *not discerning the Lord's body.*
> *For this reason many are weak and*
> *sickly among you, and many sleep.*
> *For if we would judge ourselves,*
> *we should not be judged."*
> *1Corinthians 11:28-31*

## Lack of spiritual judgement among the Corinthians

The apostle Paul was disappointed in the lack of spiritual discernment and judgement among the Corinthians, who were taking each other to the secular courts instead of having wisdom to judge between themselves.

*"I say this to your shame.*
*Is it so, that there is not a wise man*
*among you, not even one,*
*who will able to judge between his brethren?*
*But brother goes to law against brother,*
*and that before the unbelievers!"*
*1Corinthians 6:5-6*

## The Church is to judge sin and non-Biblical conduct

It is a commonly held view today, even in the church, that "real Christians do not judge others".

This of course is completely wrong thinking because the Bible actually teaches believers to "*judge all things*" (1Corinthians 2:15); beginning with the judgement of self (Matthew 7:5) and then the judgement of other believers within the church (1Corinthians 6:5).

However, the Bible does teach that Christians are not to judge non-believers, because God is their judge.

> *"I wrote to you in my epistle not to*
> *company with sexually immoral people.*
> *Yet I certainly did not mean with the*
> *sexually immoral people of this world,*
> *or with the covetous, or*
> *extortioners, or idolaters,*
> *since then would need to go out of the world.*
> *But now I have written to you*
> *not to keep company*
> *with anyone that is named a brother,*
> *who is sexually immoral, or covetous,*
> *or an idolater, or a reviler, or a*
> *drunkard, or an extortioner -*
> *not even to eat with such a person.*
> *For what have I to do with judging*
> *those also who are outside?*
> *Do you not judge those who are inside?*
> *But those who are outside God judges.*
> *Therefore "put away from*
> *yourselves the evil person".*"
> *1Corinthians 5:9-13*

The apostle Paul confirmed this judgement in the church when he stated that he had already judged a believer in the Corinthian church who was guilty of adultery.

> *"It is actually reported that there is*
> *sexual immorality among you,*
> *and such sexual immorality as is not*
> *even named among the Gentiles*
> *-that a man has his father's wife!*
> *And you are puffed up, and*
> *have not rather mourned,*
> *that he who has done this deed*
> *might be taken away from you.*
> *For I indeed, as absent in body*
> *but present in spirit,*
> *have **already judged**, (as though I were present)*
> *him who has so done this deed."*
> *1Corinthians 5:1-3*

## A life of discernment and *"spiritual understanding"*

The normal Christian lives abounding in spiritual wisdom and revelation in the power of the Holy Spirit, rather than struggling through life with the limitations of his own natural, limited understanding and abilities.

> *"That the God of our Lord Jesus*
> *Christ, the Father of glory,*
> *may give to you the spirit of wisdom and*
> *revelation in the knowledge of Him:*
> *The eyes of your understanding*
> *being enlightened;*
> *that you might know what is*
> *the hope of His calling,*
> *and what the riches of the glory of*
> *His inheritance in the saints,*
> *And what is the exceeding greatness of*
> *His power toward us who believe,*
> *according to the working of*
> *His mighty power..."*
> *Ephesians 1:17-19*

The Holy Spirit is sent by God to guide the spiritual person into "*all truth*". This results in a life of discernment and "*spiritual understanding*".

> *"However, when He, the Spirit*
> *of truth, has come,*
> *He will guide you into all truth."*
> *John 16:13*

**The normal Christian life is an unlimited life**

**There is no limit or restriction placed
on the level of revelation,
understanding and experience
for the spiritual person in Christ!**

The Scriptural limitless qualities of the *'normal Christian' are:-*

**1. We can *"KNOW (ALL) THE THINGS THAT HAVE
BEEN FREELY GIVEN TO US BY GOD"*!**

*"Now we have received, not
the spirit of the world,
but the spirit which is of God;
that we might know the things that
are freely given to us of God."
1Corinthians 2:12*

**2. We can *"DO ALL THINGS THROUGH CHRIST WHO
STRENGTHENS US"*!**

*"I can do all things through Christ
which strengthens me."
Philippians 4:13*

## 3. We can "*KNOW THAT ALL THINGS WORK TOGETHER FOR GOOD FOR THOSE WHO LOVE GOD*"!

> *"And we know that all things work together*
> *for good to them that love God,*
> *to them who are the called*
> *according to his purpose."*
> *Romans 8:28*

## 4. We can "*ABOUND IN EVERY GOOD WORK*" because God has given us "*ALL SUFFICIENCY IN ALL THINGS*"!

> *"And God is able to make all*
> *grace abound toward you;*
> *that you, always having all*
> *sufficiency in all things,*
> *may abound to every good work."*
> *2Corinthians 9:8*

## 5. We are constantly "*REACHING FORWARD TO THOSE THINGS WHICH ARE AHEAD*" IN OUR "*UPWARD CALL OF GOD*" IN OUR LIMITLESS FUTURE"!

> *"I do not count myself to have apprehended;*

*but one thing I do, forgetting those*
*things which are behind,*
*and reaching forward to those*
*things which are ahead,*
*I press toward the goal for the prize*
*of the upward call of God in Christ Jesus."*
*Philippians 3:13-14*

## The Spiritual person possesses divine wisdom to understand the Word of God

The truths of the Word of God are "*hidden*" from the '**natural man**', whose "*eyes are blinded*" (2Corinthians 4:4) and "*mind darkened*" (Ephesians 4:18). Therefore, the truths of God's Word are unknown to him and are even "*foolishness to him*" (1Corinthians 2:14).

## It is normal for the spiritual person to know the truths of God's Word

The spiritual person possesses the gift of divine wisdom and spiritual understanding. Therefore, it is normal for the spiritual person to know the truths of God's Word by revelation and by experience. This is because the truths of God's Word are "*spiritually discerned*".

*"Which things also we speak,*
*not in the words which man's wisdom teaches,*

> *but which the Holy Spirit teaches;*
> *comparing spiritual things with spiritual."*
> *1Corinthians 2:13*

As a result, the spiritual person is filled with the Word of God because the Word of God "*abides*", or lives in him.

> *"If you abide in me, and my words abide in you,*
> *you will ask what you will, and*
> *it shall be done to you."*
> *John 15:7*

## The Spiritual person is "*spiritually minded*" and is therefore full of "*life and peace*"

> *"For those who live according to the flesh*
> *set their minds on the things of the flesh,*
> *but those who live according to the Spirit,*
> *the things of the Spirit.*
> *For to be carnally minded is death;*
> *but to be spiritually minded is life and peace.*
> *Because the carnal mind is enmity against God;*
> *for it is not subject to the law of*
> *God, nor indeed can be.*
> *So then, those who are in the*
> *flesh cannot please God.*

*But you are not in the flesh, but in the Spirit,*
*if indeed the Spirit of God dwells in you."*
*Romans 8:5-9*

## The spiritual person is renewed daily

The spiritual person is being continually renewed daily in their mind and heart by the Holy Spirit and the Word of God.

*"For which cause we faint not;*
*but though our outward man perish,*
*yet the inward man is renewed day by day."*
*2Corinthians 4:17*

This provision of constant, inward renewal is so that the spiritual person will not be distracted or discouraged by the world, the flesh, or the devil. This "*daily renewing of the inner man*" keeps the spiritual person focused on what is "*the mind of the Spirit*".

The result? "**LIFE AND PEACE**"!

## The Spiritual person joins with other likeminded spiritual people - the local church

All spiritual people are born of the Holy Spirit by the same heavenly Father, have the same renewed nature, are "*spiritually minded*" and are seeking to please God in everything.

It is therefore normal for the spiritual person to seek out and to be constantly in the company of other spiritual and likeminded people.

## We have the mind of Christ

This is the local Church. This is where the spiritual person is found with other spiritually minded people and where they are mutually encouraged and discover together the 'corporate mind of Christ'.

> *"For who has known the mind of the*
> *Lord, that he may instruct him?*
> *But **WE** have the mind of Christ."*
> *1Corinthians 2:16*

Paul's statement "***we have the mind of Christ***" is important to note. This is because no single Christian by themselves possesses the fullness of God's mind and wisdom, it is only known together, hence, "**we**".

He also declared that the saints might know the love of Christ:-

*"…may be able to comprehend*
**with all the saints**
*what is the width and length and height-*
*to know the love of Christ which*
*passes all knowledge."*
*Ephesians 3:18-19*

And to be "**filled with all the fullness of God**"!

*"That you may be filled with*
*all the fullness of God."*
*Ephesians 3:19*

The apostles' revelation was that this would all result in the church bringing glory to God because the fullness of the revelation of Christ was found in the church!

*"To Him be glory **in the church** by Christ Jesus*
*to all generations."*
*Ephesians 3:21*

## The manifold wisdom of God is found in the church

The apostle Paul called this fullness of the revelation of Christ the "***manifold wisdom of God***", which would be known by the church, not the individual Christian.

> *"To the intent that now **the manifold wisdom of God might be known by the church** to the principalities and powers in heavenly places."*
> *Ephesians 3:10*

## The many-coloured wisdom of God

The choice of the word "*manifold*" by the apostle Paul is used to show that "*God's wisdom is many and varied; having many features and forms*" (gotquestions.org).

This is the "***many-coloured wisdom of God***" (Barclay's Translation), linking it with Joseph's "*tunic of many colours*" (Genesis 37:3).

Paul's concept is that the manifold wisdom of God can only be fully discovered in the Body of Christ in the local church, where all the members are united together in faith.

*"Till we all come to the unity of the faith*
*and of the knowledge of the Son of God".*
*Ephesians 4:13*

## Each member of the Body possesses part of God's wisdom

Each member of the Body of Christ possesses a different aspect and part of God's wisdom and knowledge. Together the church is embroidered, or "**knit together**" (Colossians 2:19), by the Spirit of God to create the "*coat of many colours*" of "*the manifold wisdom of God*" in the church.

*"There are **diversities of gifts**,*
*but the same Spirit.*
*There are **differences of ministries**,*
*but the same Lord.*
*There are **diversities of activities**, but it*
*is the same God who works all in all.*
*But the manifestation of the Spirit **is given***
***to each one** for the profit of all."*
*1Corinthians 12:4-7*

## Each member is to minister *"for the profit of all."*

Each member has a contribution to make towards the edification and building up of the Body of Christ from their personal revelation, gifts and experience.

> *"How is it then, brethren?*
> *Whenever you come together,*
> ***each of you has*** *a psalm,*
> *has a teaching, has a tongue, has a*
> *revelation, has an interpretation.*
> *Let all things be done for edification."*
> *1Corinthians 14:26*

Each member is to be filled with the Word of God *"in all wisdom"*. This will cause an overflow in *"teaching and admonishing one another"* so the church is encouraged, strengthened and built up.

> *"Let the word of Christ dwell in*
> *you richly in all wisdom;*
> ***teaching and admonishing one another***
> *in psalms and hymns and spiritual songs,*
> *singing with grace in your hearts to the Lord."*
> *Colossians 3:16*

## The leaders of the church articulate the *"manifold wisdom of God"* to the church

The leaders of the church have been given a special God given role to communicate the "manifold wisdom of God" to the church. This is achieved through:-

### 1. The foundational ministry of the apostles and prophets

> *"Having been built on **the foundation**
> **of the apostles and prophets**,
> Jesus Christ Himself being the
> chief corner stone,
> in whom the whole building,
> being fitted together,
> grows into a holy temple in the Lord."*
> *Ephesians 2:20*

### 2. The apostles doctrine

> *"And they continued steadfastly in the
> **apostles' doctrine** and fellowship,
> in breaking of bread, and in prayers."*
> *Act 2:42*

## 3. The preaching and teaching of apostles

*"And **my speech and my preaching**
were not with persuasive words
of human wisdom,
but in demonstration of the Spirit and of power,
That your faith should not be in the wisdom
of men but in the power of God."*
*1Corinthians 2:4*

## 4. The equipping and edifying of the saints by leaders

*"And He Himself gave some to be
apostles, some, prophets,
some evangelists, and some
pastors and teachers,*
***for the equipping of the saints
for the work of ministry,
for the edifying of the body of Christ:***
*Till we all come to the unity of the faith,
and of the knowledge of the Son of God,
to a perfect man, to the measure of the
stature of the fullness of Christ."*
*Ephesians 4:11-12*

## 5. The preaching of the leaders

*"But now, brethren, if I come to
you speaking with tongues,
what shall I profit you unless **I speak
to you** either by revelation,
by knowledge, by prophesying, or by teaching?"
1Corinthians 14:6*

## 6. The teaching of the bishops

*"A bishop then must be blameless,
the husband of one wife,
temperate, sober-minded,
of good behaviour, hospitable, **able to teach.**"
1Timothy 3:2*

## 7. The preaching and teaching of travelling ministers

*"who have borne witness of your
love before the church.
If you send them forward on their
journey in a manner worthy,
you will do well, because they went
forth for His name's sake,
taking nothing from the Gentiles.
We therefore ought to receive such,*

> *that we may become **fellow***
> ***workers for the truth.** "*
> *3John 6-8*

## The Spiritual person is growing in maturity

In order to correct divisions that had entered the Corinthian church the apostle Paul draws a comparison between those who are "*spiritual"*, or mature, and those who are "*babes*", or immature. This is because immature Christians tend to act irresponsibly with a spirit of divisiveness.

On the other hand, the spiritual quality of maturity is unity, or oneness.

> *"However brothers and sisters,*
> *I could not talk to you as to spiritual people,*
> *but [only] as to worldly people*
> *[dominated by human nature],*
> *mere infants [in the new life] in Christ!*
> *1 Corinthians 3:1 Amplified Bible*

As a result, the spiritually mature person is building the unity of the believers, not tearing it down!

*"Until we all reach oneness in the faith and*
*in the knowledge of the Son of God,*
*[growing spiritually] to become*
*a mature believer,*
*reaching to the measure of the fullness of Christ*
*[manifesting His spiritual completeness and*
*exercising our spiritual gifts in unity]."*
*Ephesians 4:13 Amplified Bible*

This spiritual *"unity"* and *"oneness"* results in us *"grow(ing) up into Him in all things"*

*"That we should no longer be **children**,*
*tossed to and fro and carried about*
*with every wind of doctrine,*
*by the trickery of men, in the cunning*
*craftiness of deceitful plotting,*
***But, speaking the truth in love, may***
***grow up in all things into Him***
*who is the head, even Christ."*
*Ephesians 4:14-15*

The writer of Hebrews uses the same idea with the word "*babe*", referring to believers who have not grown in their spiritual knowledge and understanding sufficiently and so cannot be "*teachers*" of others.

*"Of whom we have much to say,*
*and hard to explain, since you have*
*become dull of hearing.*
*For though by this time you*
*ought to be teachers,*
*you need someone to teach you again*
*the first principles of the oracles of God;*
*and you have come to need*
*milk and not solid food.*
*For anyone who partakes only of milk is*
*unskilled in the word of righteousness,*
*for he is a babe.*
*But solid food belongs to those*
*that are of full age,*
*that is, those who by reason of use*
*have their senses exercised to*
*discern both good and evil."*
*Hebrews 5:11-14*

**The spiritual person possesses the boldness to speak those things that have been freely given by God**

*"Now we have received, not*
*the spirit of the world,*
*but the Spirit who is from God;*
*that we might know the things that have*

*been freely given to us by God.*
***These things also we speak****, not in*
*words which man's wisdom teaches*
*but which the Holy Spirit teaches,*
*comparing spiritual things with spiritual."*
*1Corinthians 2:12-13*

*"That which we have seen and*
*heard **we declare to you**,*
*that ye also may have fellowship with us:*
*and truly our fellowship is with the*
*Father, and with his Son Jesus Christ.*
*And these things write we unto*
*you, that your joy may be full.*
*This then is the message which*
*we have heard of Him,*
*and **declare to you**,*
*that God is light, and in Him*
*is no darkness at all."*
*1John 1:3-5*

**"Because the Bible tells the spiritual man**
**his position and condition,**
**he is at liberty to say what God says he is,**
**and has, and can do in Christ"**
**H Greenwood**

## The spiritual person is living in the overflow of the Word of God and the Holy Spirit to minister to others

The spiritual person is filled to overflow with the Word of God and the Holy Spirit. Therefore, there is more than enough provision flowing out from the '*normal Christian*' to meet his needs and to minister to the needs of others.

*"And do not be drunk with wine,*
*in which is dissipation;*
*but be filled with the Spirit,*
***speaking*** *to one another in psalms*
*and hymns and spiritual songs,*
*singing and making melody in*
*your heart to the Lord."*
*Ephesians 5:18-19*

*"Let the Word of Christ dwell in*
*you richly in all wisdom,*
***teaching*** *and* ***admonishing*** *one another*
*in psalms and hymns and spiritual songs,*
*singing with grace in your hearts to the Lord."*
*Colossians 3:16*

This is the fullness of the Holy Spirit, the fullness of the gospel and the fullness of God!

The normal Christian lives and ministers in the "*fullness*" that God supplies in Christ.

> *"And I am sure that, when I come unto you,*
> *I shall come in the fulness of the*
> *blessing of the gospel of Christ."*
> *Romans 15:29*

> *"And to know the love of Christ,*
> *which passes knowledge,*
> *that you might be filled with*
> *all the fulness of God."*
> *Ephesians 3:19*

## Free, able and fully resourced to give: a blessing to others

Because the spiritual person is living a life of fullness and overflow he is free, able and fully resourced to give. The spiritual person is constantly reaching out to meet the needs of others because he is living by faith in divine supply and is therefore able to minister freely and generously to others.

> *"And as you go, preach, saying,*
> *The kingdom of heaven is at hand.*

> *Heal the sick, cleanse the lepers,*
> *raise the dead, cast out devils:*
> ***freely*** *you have **received**, **freely give**. "*
> *Matthew 10:7-8*

The 'normal Christian' is not seeking to be blessed because he is **already blessed** with "*every spiritual blessing in Christ*" (Ephesians 1:3).

This is why the focus for the spiritual person is about **being a blessing to others** who are not blessed or living in God's abundant provision in Christ.

**THE SPIRITUAL PERSON HAS EVERYTHING THEY NEED IN CHRIST. THEY ALREADY HAVE AN OVERFLOW OF THE HOLY SPIRIT OUT OF WHAT THEY HAVE ALREADY RECEIVED FROM GOD!**

There is no concern of lack, or a sense of withholding or conserving because the spiritual person is living in the abundance and overflow of God.

## The spiritual person is not limited or restricted in ministering to others

The spiritual person isn't limited or restricted in ministering to others because he lacks certain gifts or abilities, or resources, or the need is too big for him.

Rather, because he is already filled with the Holy Spirit in fulness he believes that he's filled with all the Holy Spirit's provision for any need or situation.

Therefore, the spiritual person simply trusts in the leading and the ability of the Holy Spirit to meet whatever need might arise.

## Giving is seed in the ground

The '*normal Christian*' continually gives and contributes generously to others because he knows that his giving is "*seed in the ground*" and will return to him in an abundant harvest!

*"There is who that scatters, yet increases more;*
*and there is one who withholds*
*more than is right,*
*but it leads to poverty.*

*The generous soul will be made rich:*
*and he who waters will also be watered himself."*
*Proverbs 11:24-25*

**The spiritual person recognises**
**that God got all these things TO HIM,**
**so God could get all these things**
**THROUGH HIM to others!**

The greatest blessing is in the giving not in the receiving.
This is the mindset and lifestyle of the '*normal Christian*'!

*"Remember the words of the*
*Lord Jesus, that He said,*
***It is more blessed to give than to receive.***"
*Acts 20:35*

**THE SPIRITUAL PERSON**
**LIVES IN HIS GIVING.**
**HE IS SIMPLY LIVING IN THE HARVEST**
**AND RESULTS OF HIS GIVING!**

## The lifestyle of the Spiritual person

What does the 'normal' lifestyle of the spiritual person
look like?

The Cambridge Dictionary describes lifestyle as "**someone's way of living**". Therefore,

'Lifestyle' is the attitudes, values, approach, mindset and mode of operation of a person's life.

The spiritual person's attitude and approach is not one of trying to be brave and confident through self-motivation, or positive thinking to cope with fear, confusion, lack and intimidation. He already has a spirit of power, love and a sound mind given to him by God!

*"For God has not given us the spirit of fear;*
*but of power, and of love, and of a sound mind."*
*2Tim 1:7*

## The spiritual person lives normally in constant victory

Because the spiritual person is a new creation in Christ he finds that it is 'more normal' to live in victory than in defeat! Therefore, the spiritual person naturally believes that he *"can do all the things through Christ who strengthens me!" (Philippians 4:13)*

**The normal Christian has internal rivers and a well of living water in him flowing out from his heart**

He is living by the internal presence and power of the Holy Spirit within him and is not looking for an external source of spiritual life.

*"He who believes in Me, as*
*the Scripture has said,*
*out of his heart will flow rivers of living water."*
*John 7:38*
*"But whoever drinks of the water that*
*I shall give him will never thirst.*
*But the water that I shall give*
*him will become in him*
*a well of water springing up*
*into everlasting life."*
*John 4:14*

As a result, the spiritual person is not trying to get closer to Christ because he already has Christ living in him by faith!

*"I am crucified with Christ: nevertheless I live;*
*yet not I, but **Christ lives in me**:*
*and the life that I now live in the flesh*
*I live by faith in the Son of God,*

*who loved me, and gave Himself for me."*
*Galatians 2:20*

## The '*normal Christian*' cannot claim what he ALREADY POSSESSES in Christ!

The '*normal Christian*' cannot get what he already has or claim what he already possesses in Christ!

The provision of Christ's salvation is perfect and complete. Therefore, the '*normal Christian*' has all he needs in Christ for all time and every situation!

*"For in Him dwells all the fulness*
*of the Godhead bodily.*
*And you are complete in Him."*
*Colossians 2:9-10*

As a result, the spiritual person simply believes, speaks, acts and lives by faith in the complete and perfect provision of Christ that he already possesses!

This provision of Christ is very near to the spiritual person: in his mouth and in his heart.

*"But the righteousness of faith*
*speaks in this way,*

*Do not in your heart, 'Who will*
*ascend into heaven?*
*(that is, to bring Christ down from above)*
*or, Who will descend into the abyss?*
*(that is, to bring Christ up from the dead).*
*But what does it say?*
*The word is near you, in your*
*mouth, and in your heart*
*(that is, the word of faith, which we preach)."*
*Romans 10:6-8*

**The normal Christian is constantly growing and progressing in what he already possesses in Christ**

*"Meditate upon these things; give*
*yourself entirely to them;*
*that your progress may be evident to all."*
*1Timothy 4:15*

For example, the '*normal Christian*' is not trying to get or find more grace, but rather is growing and progressing every day in the grace of God which he already possesses in Christ!

*"But grow in grace, and in the knowledge*
*of our Lord and Saviour Jesus Christ.*
*To Him be glory both now and for ever. Amen"*
*2Peter 3:18*

## The '*normal Christian*' believes he cannot lose what he already possesses in Christ!

The spiritual person believes that he can never be separated from the love, presence and provision of God because he already possesses *"Christ in you the hope of glory" (Colossians 1:27)*.

As he lives and walks daily in the presence of God by faith he is being renewed, strengthened and progressed by the Holy Spirit in the inner man.

*"For I am persuaded, that neither*
*death, nor life, nor angels,*
*nor principalities, nor powers, nor*
*things present, nor things to come,*
*Nor height, nor depth, nor any other creature,*
*shall be able to separate us*
*from the love of God,*
*which is in Christ Jesus our Lord."*
*Romans 8:38-39*

## The 'normal Christian' life is unwaveringly steadfast

*"Therefore, lay aside all filthiness*
*and overflow of wickedness,*

*and receive with meekness the implanted word,*
*which is able to save your souls."*
*James 1:21*

The use of the word "*implanted*", or "*engrafted*", is from the Greek word "*emphutos*" (Strongs Concordance, G1721) which means "*inborn, implanted by nature*".

The precise choice of this word by the Scriptures is used to convey the depth, strength and solidity of the implanted Word of God within the new nature of the disciple of Christ.

This is what makes it normal for the '*normal Christian*' to be "*steadfast and immovable*" in their faith!

*"But thanks be to God,*
*Who gives us the victory through*
*our Lord Jesus Christ.*
*Therefore, my beloved brethren,*
*be steadfast, immovable,*
*always abounding in the work of the Lord,*
*forasmuch as you know that your*
*labour is not in vain in the Lord."*
*1Corinthians 15:57-58*

The writer to the Hebrews expresses this same idea when he uses the nautical phrase "*anchor to the soul*", which is "*both sure and steadfast*".

> *"This hope we have as an anchor of*
> *the soul, both sure and stedfast,*
> *and which enters the Presence behind the veil."*
> Hebrews 6:19

Again, this is declaring the depth, solidarity and strength of the '*normal Christian's*' faith because the Word of God has been deeply "*implanted*", or "*engrafted*", in his heart.

## The normal Christian is born supernaturally and lives supernaturally through the undying Word of God

The natural person is born of "*corruptible seed", the* flesh, and will die. By comparison, the '*normal Christian*' is born of the "*incorruptible seed*" of the eternal, undying and abiding Word of God, and will never die!

> *"Being born again, not of corruptible*
> *seed, but of incorruptible,*
> *by the Word of God, which lives*
> *and abides for ever."*
> *1Peter 1:23*

**The normal Christian lives supernaturally by faith in victory, confidence and empowerment**

The *"implanted, incorruptible Word of God"* creates the spiritual person, who now finds it more normal to live supernaturally by faith in victory, confidence and empowerment - THIS IS NORMAL CHRISTIANITY!

> *"For whatever is born of God*
> *overcomes the world.*
> *And this is the victory that has*
> *overcome the world-our faith.*
> *1John 5:4*

> **"The spiritual man is the divine**
> **ideal in life and ministry,**
> **in power with God and man,**
> **in unbroken fellowship and blessing."**
> **Lewis Sherry Chafer**

**The normal Christian is rightly relating to the Holy Spirit**

He who is spiritual is more than a mere Christian, who just believes in Christ. The spiritual person is rightly relating to the Holy Spirit in his whole life!

1.  Born of the Spirit (John 3:3)
2.  In dwelt by the Spirit (1 Corinthians 3:16)
3.  Filled with the Spirit (Ephesians 4:18)
4.  Sanctified in the Spirit (1 Corinthians 6:11)
5.  Justified in the Spirit (1 Corinthians 6:11)
6.  Led by the Spirit (Romans 8:14)
7.  Bearing witness with the Spirit (Romans 8:16)
8.  Strengthened in the Spirit (Ephesians 3:16)
9.  Renewed daily in the Spirit (Ephesians 423)
10. Given the manifestation of the Spirit (1 Corinthians 12:7)
11. Living in the Spirit (Galatians 5:25)
12. Walking in the Spirit (Galatians 5:25)
13. Praying in the Spirit (Ephesians 6:18)
14. Ministering in the Spirit (1 Corinthians 2:4)
15. Worshipping God in the Spirit (Philippians 3:3)

## The normal Christian has judgement and spiritual discernment regarding sin

The apostle Paul was disappointed when he identified the lack of judgement and spiritual discernment regarding sin among the Corinthians. He stated that the lack of judgement and self examination was as one of the main reasons for spiritual "*weakness, sickness and even sleep, or death.*"

*"But let a man examine himself,
and so let him eat of the bread,
and drink of the cup.
For he who eats and drinks in
an unworthy manner,
eats and drinks judgement to himself,
not discerning the Lord's body.
For this reason many are weak and
sick among you, and many sleep.
For if we would judge ourselves,
we would not be judged."
1Corinthians 11:28-31*

Spiritual apathy, sickness and even death is never a consideration for the spiritual person because he is always alive to God by the power of the Holy Spirit!

*"And if Christ is in you, the body
is dead because of sin;
but the Spirit is life because of righteousness.
For if you live according to the flesh, you will die;
but if by the Spirit you put to death the
deeds of the body, you will live."
Romans 8:10,13*

## So why do we have (and need) revivals?

The spiritual person is not waiting for or needing a revival to make himself more spiritually alive, or to be closer to God because he is living constantly with the life giving Spirit of God within him!

However to a dead person revival is very important because to be revived means to come back to life! A 'revivalist' is constantly looking for and needing a revival because they, or someone else, or something is spiritually 'dead', or 'asleep'.

This is why there is always a need for revivals throughout history and especially in our generation. Christians can grow lukewarm, apathetic and even die spiritually and especially in the present hedonistic age of relativism and materialism.

*"I know your works, that you*
*are neither cold nor hot.*
*I could wish you were cold or hot.*
*So then, because you are lukewarm,*
*and neither cold nor hot,*
*I will vomit you out of My mouth.*
*Because you say, I am rich, have become*
*wealthy, and and have need of nothing-*

*and do not know that you are wretched,
miserable, poor, blind and naked."
Revelation 3:15-17*

A spiritual person believes in and promotes 'moves of God' and "*Times of Restoration*" (Acts 3:21) that revive Christians and progressively restore truth, but not to revive an already "*alive in Christ*" person!

*"Likewise reckon yourselves to
be dead indeed unto sin,
but alive to God through Jesus Christ our Lord."
Romans 6:11*

## Revivals are important and exciting

Revivals are important and exciting when they happen because they renew and revive what is lost or dead. Spiritual zeal and fervour for God is ignited by revival as God's people return to their "*first love*" (Revelation 2:4).

**Revival is bringing a person back
to where they should be in the
first place - ALIVE TO GOD!**

However, revivals never last because they're not supposed to! Revivals occur in order to bring people back to where they should be in the first place…ALIVE TO GOD!

> *"The tendency of fire is to go out;*
> *watch the fire on the altar of your heart.*
> *Anyone who has tended a fireplace fire*
> *knows that it needs to be*
> *stirred up occasionally."*
> *General William Booth*

A spiritual person promotes the need for revival because he knows the importance of God's people being restored and made alive in God. Revival will empower the church to be passionate and busy about the Lord's work of building the Church: winning lost people, making disciples and growing leaders.

> *"Therefore, my beloved brethren,*
> *be stedfast, immovable, always*
> *abounding in the work of the Lord,*
> *knowing that your labour is*
> *not in vain in the Lord."*
> *1Corinthians 15:58*

## Revived to live by faith

Once a revival has been effected, God's people are called to "*live by faith*" as spiritual people; dead to sin and alive to God in the power of the Holy Spirit and in the Word of God!

> *"For in it the righteousness of God*
> *revealed from faith to faith;*
> *as it is written, "The just shall live by faith"."*
> *Romans 1:17*

## Chapter Four

# THE GOD WHO SEES ME

This abundant life that God has prepared for us is not limited by our humanity, lacks, faults or inabilities. It is a brand new life in the Holy Spirit which God has provided for us in Jesus Christ.

This new life in Christ is ever unfolding, progressive and advancing; a 'beyond life'. When we discover it we will find ourselves living above and beyond our own thinking, feelings and needs. We will be living in the overflow of Christ's provision. This is how God sees us!

### GOD HAS A MUCH BIGGER IDEA ABOUT YOU THAN YOU COULD IMAGINE!

This is what the apostle Paul realised. God's 'big idea' about His children has not been seen by human eyes, or heard by human ears, or even entered into human hearts. This big idea is God's idea, it is God's plan and will for our lives!

> *"But as it is written, eye has*
> *not seen, nor ear heard,*
> *neither has it entered into the heart of man,*
> *the things that God has prepared*
> *for them that love him.»*
> *1Corinthians 2:9*

When we consider God's great purpose for us we can identify three key characteristics.

## 1. We are Designed for Likeness

> *"And God said, Let us make man in*
> *our **image**, after our **likeness**...»*
> *Genesis 1:26-28*

To be created in the "*image*" and "*likeness*" of God means that we are like God. This is our innate, created purpose. This is because we carry God's image and likeness 'naturally'. In other words, it is "*unconditioned, unlearned, inborn and not established by conditioning or learning*" (CED).

When God created us in His image and likeness we were designed to be different from all of creation. We were designed to have fellowship with God. This is because God values people and therefore, He values relationships.

God breathed life into Adam alone, which gave him God's spiritual life along with his natural, physical life. This is what sets humans apart from all of creation.

This innate, inborn likeness and image gifted humans with:-

* **MORAL, FREE CHOICE -** to know right and wrong by conscience and thought and to choose freely to do good, or evil.
* **SPEECH -** communication beyond instinct and response to intimacy, ideas, logic and values.
* **CREATIVE, IMAGINATIVE INTELLIGENCE -** the ability to think logically, to reason, see, envision, imagine possibilities and create.

## 2. We are Destined for Greatness

*"And let them have **DOMINION**
over the fish of the sea,
and over the fowl of the air, and over
the cattle, and over all the earth,
and over every creeping thing*

*that creeps upon the earth.*
*So God created man in His own image,*
*in the image of God created He him;*
*male and female created He them.*
*And God **BLESSED** them,*
*and God said to them, Be **FRUITFUL**,*
*and **MULTIPLY**, and **REPLENISH***
*the earth, and **SUBDUE** it."*
*Genesis 1:26-28*

From this declaration by God at creation we can identify the following attributes He gave humans:

We were created by God:

- \*    To have **DOMINION**
- \*    To be **BLESSED**
- \*    To be **FRUITFUL**
- \*    To **MULTIPLY**
- \*    To **FILL THE EARTH**
- \*    To **SUBDUE THE EARTH**

### 3.  We are Delivered for Eternity

We were not destined to just live for 80 years on the earth and that's it! We were created by God to live forever in fellowship with Him.

This was lost at the fall of Adam and Eve but restored in Christ's accomplishments at the Cross.

## God's knowledge, calling and love for us preceded our existence!

*"Before I formed you in the belly **I knew you**;*
*and before you came forth out of*
*the womb **I sanctified you**,*
*and **I ordained you** a prophet unto the nations."*
*Jeremiah 1:5*

*"Your eyes saw my substance,*
*yet being unformed;*
*and in Your book they were written,*
*the days fashioned for me, **when as***
***yet there were none of them**."*
*Ps 139:16*

## God saw us before we existed

David spoke of God's all-knowing and all-seeing ability when He saw him as a human being in the womb and had a plan for his life.

*"**Your eyes saw me** when I
was inside the womb.
All the days ordained for me
were recorded in your scroll
**before one of them came into existence**."
(NET)*

## God's knowledge of us precedes our conception

Jeremiah heard the Lord declare that He knew Jeremiah before he was formed, or existed! This also included Jeremiah's appointment to his calling as a prophet.

*"Before I formed you in the womb I knew you;
and before you we're born I consecrated you,
and I appointed you a prophet to the nations."
Jeremiah 1:5 ESV*

The apostle Paul also declared God's knowledge of us before we existed.

*"For whom He foreknew,
He also predestined to be conformed
to the image of His Son,
that He might be the firstborn
among many brethren."
Romansh 8:29*

## God's thoughts toward us are countless as the sand on the seashore

The psalmist tells us that God's thoughts toward us even outnumber the grains of sand on the seashore!

> *"How difficult it is for me to fathom*
> *your thoughts about me, O God!*
> *How vast is their sum total!*
> *If I tried to count them,*
> *they would outnumber the grains of sand.*
> *Even if I finished counting them,*
> *I would still have to contend with you."*
> *Ps 139:17-18 (NET)*

What imagery! How unfathomable for us to grasp this concept that we have always been in God's mind and in His heart!

Our heavenly Father is thinking about His children all the time and they are not thoughts of condemnation and judgement. They are thoughts of love, hope, success and destiny!

> *"For I know what I have planned*
> *for you,' says the Lord.*
> *'I have plans to prosper you, not to harm you.*

*I have plans to give you a*
*future filled with hope."*
*Jeremiah 29:11 (NET)*

## God is for us, not against us

*"What then shall we say about these things?*
*If God is for us, who can be against us?*
*Indeed, He who did not spare His own Son,*
*but gave Him up for us all – how will He not also,*
*along with Him, freely give us all things?"*
*Romans 8:31-32 (NET)*

## GOD'S LOVE FOR HIS CHILDREN IS ETERNAL

*"Behold, what manner of love the*
*Father has bestowed upon us,*
*that we should be called the sons of God:*
*therefore the world knows us not,*
*because it knew him not.*
*Beloved, now are we the sons of God, and*
*it does not yet appear what we shall be:*
*but we know that, when he shall*
*appear, we shall be like him;*
*for we shall see him as he is.*

*And every man that hath this hope in him
purifies himself, even as he is pure."
1John 3:1-3*

## OUR GOD
## IS THE GOD
## WHO SEES US!

## Chapter Five

# I AM WHO GOD SAYS I AM

What we say and do flows out of who we think we are. Who we think we are forms our sense of identity, or self-image and self-worth. Everything in life flows from this.

> *"For as he **thinks** in his heart, **so is he**."*
> *Proverbs 23:7*

Therefore, whatever *'treasure'*, or lack, that is in our hearts we will bring out into our lives.

## GOOD TREASURE IN OUR HEART = GOOD THINGS IN OUR LIFE!

*"A good man out of the good treasure of his heart brings forth that which is good; and an evil man out of the evil treasure of his heart brings forth that which is evil:*

*for out of the abundance of the*
*heart his mouth speaks."*
*Luke 6:45*

## WHATEVER IS IN OUR HEARTS
## WILL EVENTUALLY COME OUT IN OUR LIVES

This is why the book of Proverbs instructs us to "*keep our hearts with all diligence*" because our lives are flowing out from our hearts; out of what we believe.

*"Keep your heart with all diligence;*
*for out of it spring the issues of life."*
*Proverbs 4:23*

When we have a clear and vivid picture on the inside of our God given image and identity we will live according to that vision.

### We are created in the image and likeness of God.

Just like Adam and Eve, we are created naturally in the likeness and image of God. We were also created spiritually by the new birth to be like Him in:-

* **attributes** – a free, moral being, intellectual person

* **character** – a righteous, loving, faith-filled, generous and kind person
* **nature** – a person who lives a life of dominion, fruitfulness, increase, progress and creativity

The Bible states that of all God's creatures only human beings were created in the express image of God. This concept is from the Latin "*imago Dei*", meaning "*divine image*".

Therefore, every individual person possesses inherent dignity, moral worth, and eternal value to God!

## Our value is determined by God

Our value as a person is not determined by our past, by what we do, or don't do. Our value was decided by God when He created us in His image!

Every human being possesses this inherent dignity, moral worth, and eternal value to God above all of His creation!

*"Look at the birds of the air:*
*for they neither sow nor reap*
*nor gather into barns;*
*yet your heavenly Father feeds them.*
***Are you not of more value than they***?*"*
*Matthew 6:26*

Therefore, our existence, value and meaning are intrinsically linked to our Father in heaven! We are who He says we are!

> *"But as many as received Him*
> *to them He gave the power to*
> *become children of God."*
> *John 1:12*

## The new birth creates us in God's image

In Christ we have been "**created**", "*ktizo*" (Strongs Concordance, G2936), which means to be "**completely changed and transformed**" through the new birth.

> *"For we are His workmanship [His*
> *own master work, a work of art],*
> *created in Christ Jesus [reborn from*
> *above—spiritually transformed, renewed,*
> *ready to be used] for good works, which*
> *God prepared [for us] beforehand*
> *[taking paths which He set], so*
> *that we would walk in them*
> *[living the good life which He prearranged*
> *and made ready for us]."*
> *Ephesians 2:10 Amplified Bible*

The deceit of the Devil is seen right from the beginning where he presented the biggest lie in the history of mankind, that we were not like God!

> *"For God knows that on the day you*
> *eat from it your eyes will be opened*
> *[that is, you will have greater awareness],*
> *and **you will be like God**,*
> *knowing [the difference*
> *between] good and evil."*
> *Genesis 3:5 Amplified Bible*

The reality was that Adam and Eve were **already like God**, because God had created them in His "***likeness and image***".

> *"So God created human beings*
> *in His own image,*
> *in the image of God He created them;*
> *male and female He created them."*
> *Genesis 1:27 New Living Translation*

However, Adam and Eve believed the lie of the Devil and disobeyed God. As a result, sin and death entered, marring the divine image and severing their relationship with God.

> *"But of the tree of the knowledge of*
> *good and evil, you shall not eat of it:*
> *for in the day that you eat of*
> *it you shall surely die."*
> *Genesis 2:17*

## The 'BIG elephant in the room': SIN

Ever since the garden of Eden the big issue for mankind has been and still is, sin.

> *"For all have sinned, and fall*
> *short of the glory of God."*
> *Romans 3:23*

Everyone knows it exists, but we try to avoid it, pretend it's not there, or try to reduce it's impact by redefining it. For example, sex outside marriage is defined in the Bible as "*fornication*", now it's redefined as "an affair", or "living with my partner".

## Sin separates us from God

The major problem with sin is that it separates us from God because He is holy.

*"But your iniquities have separated
between you and your God,
and your sins have hid His face from
you, that He will not hear."
Is 59:2*

**God's remedy for sin - an altar with the *"shedding of blood"***

*"And almost all things are by the
law purged with blood;
**and without shedding of
blood is no remission.**"
Hebrews 9:22*

As soon as Adam and Eve had sinned God established the first altar as the remedy for their sin. The lives of two animals were sacrificed and their skins were made into clothes by God and given to Adam and Eve to cover their nakedness.

*"And the Lord God made
clothing from animal skins
for Adam and his wife."
Genesis 3:21 NLT*

## Sin is expensive

Wherever there is sin there must be the sacrifice of a life; "*the shedding of blood*". Sin is expensive because only a life can pay for sin.

Therefore, Jesus Christ came as the "*lamb of God*" to sacrifice and provide His own "*precious blood*" to redeem us from sin.

> *"Knowing that you were not redeemed*
> *with corruptible things,*
> *like silver and gold,*
> *from your aimless conduct received*
> *by tradition from your fathers,*
> *but with the **precious blood of Christ**,*
> *as of **a lamb without blemish**
> **and without spot**."*
> *1Peter 1:18-19*

## What is sin?

The Scriptures define sin as the…

*   **TRANSGRESSION** of the law of God ("*lawlessness*")

*"Whoever commits sin transgresses also the law:*
*for sin is the **transgression of the law**."*
*1John 3:4 KJV*

*"commits lawlessness...*
***sin is lawlessness**"*
*1John 3:4 NKJV*

\*   **REBELLION** against God

*"Whoever **rebels** against your command*
*and does not heed your words, in*
*all that You command him..."*
*Josh 1:18*

\*   All **UNRIGHTEOUSNESS**

*"All unrighteousness is sin."*
*1John 5:17*

We have all sinned and we do so in two ways:-

\*   **sins of omission** - living a general lifestyle of lawlessness; a self-centred lifestyle without any thought or consideration of God and His will.
\*   **sins of commission -** specific commands in the Law that we disobey; we know what is right, but we don't do it

## Sin has wages, or consequences

*"For the wages of sin is death;*
*but the gift of God is eternal life*
*through Jesus Christ our Lord."*
*Romans 6:23*

## The fracture of sin

Sin created a '*fracture of sin*' in the human heart and psyche which resulted in the loss of our true 'God identity' and replaced "*righteousness, peace and joy*" with:-

- sin and death
- spiritual blindness
- unrighteousness
- sexual immorality
- lust
- guilt
- fear
- insecurity
- pride
- haters of God
- envy
- greed
- violence

- deceit
- untrustworthiness
- slander
- ungratefulness
- condemnation

*"Therefore God gave them up to
uncleanness, in the lusts of their hearts
to dishonour their bodies among themselves.
who exchanged the truth of God for the lie,
and worshiped and served the
creature rather than the Creator,
who is blessed forever. Amen.
For this reason God gave them
up to vile passions.
For even their women exchanged the
natural use for what is against nature.
Likewise also the men, leaving the
natural use of the women,
burned in their lust for one another,
men with men committing what is shameful
and receiving in themselves the penalty
of their error which was due.
And even as they did not like to
retain God in their knowledge,
God gave them over to a debased mind,*

*to do those things which are not fitting;
being filled with all unrighteousness, sexual
immorality, wickedness, covetousness,
maliciousness; full of envy, murder,
strife, deceit, evil-mindedness;
They are whisperers, backbiters, haters of
God, violent, proud, boasters, inventors
of evil things, disobedient to parents,
undiscerning, untrustworthy, unloving,
unforgiving, unmerciful;
who, knowing the righteous judgement of God,
that those who practice such things
are deserving of death,
not only do the same, but also approve
of those who practice them."
Romans 1:24-32*

*"Do you not know that the unrighteous
will not inherit the kingdom of God?
Do not be deceived.
Neither fornicators, nor idolaters, nor
adulterers, nor homosexuals, nor sodomites,
nor thieves, nor covetous, nor drunkards,
nor revilers, nor extortioners,
will inherit the kingdom of God.
And such were some of you.*

*But you were washed, but you were sanctified,*
*but you were justified in the*
*name of the Lord Jesus,*
*and by the Spirit of our God."*
*1Corinthians 6:9-13*

*"Now the works of the flesh*
*are evident, which are:*
*Adultery, fornication, uncleanness, lewdness,*
*Idolatry, sorcery, hatred, contentions,*
*jealousies, outbursts of wrath, selfish*
*ambitions, dissensions, heresies,*
*envy, murders, drunkenness,*
*revelries, and the like:*
*of the which I tell you beforehand, just*
*as I also told you in time past,*
*that those who practice such things will*
*not inherit the kingdom of God."*
*Galatians 5:19-21*

## The redeeming mission of Christ

The Lord Jesus Christ came to earth with the express mission of redeeming this loss and fracture of sin and death through His atoning work on the cross.

Through this act of love and grace we have been provided with the "*new birth*" which activates Christ's redemption experientially in the believer.

Sin and it's penalty of death is removed, God's image and our fellowship with God is restored. We are supernaturally made children of God by the work of the Holy Spirit.

> *"That which is born of the flesh is flesh,*
> *and that which is born of the Spirit is spirit."*
> *John 3:6*

## The new birth is the spiritual and sovereign work of the Holy Spirit

This work of God in the new birth is not through natural or human effort or agency, nor by religious means, "*not of blood, nor of the will of the flesh, nor of the will of man*" (John 1:13).

But rather, the new birth is the sovereign, spiritual and supernatural action of the Holy Spirit in response to the receiving faith of an individual.

> *"But as many as received Him,*
> *to them He gave the power to*

*become children of God,*
*to those who believe on His name:*
*who were born, not of blood,*
*nor of the will of the flesh,*
*nor of the will of man, but of God."*
*John 1:12-13*

## The new birth in Christ fully restores our 'God identity'

This supernatural "*new birth*" of the Holy Spirit restores the 'God identity' in us, because we are "*born of God*" and now carry God's "*seed*" within us, which is God's very nature, image, likeness and character.

*"Whoever is born of God does not commit sin;*
*for His seed remains in him:*
*and he cannot sin, because he is born of God."*
*1John 3:9*

Our identity is now found in the "**new man**" or the "**new creation**"; the spiritual, supernatural, regenerated, inner person in Christ Jesus.

*"Therefore, from now on, we regard*
*no one according to the flesh.*
*Even though we have known Christ*

*according to the flesh,*
*yet now we know Him thus no longer.*
*Therefore, **if any one is in Christ**,*
*he is **a new creation;***
*old things are passed away;*
*behold, **all things are become new**."*
*2Corinthians 5:16-17*

This "*new creation*" in the "*new birth*" produces God's
nature in "*righteousness and true holiness*"; the spiritual
person is created.

*"That you put off concerning*
*your former conduct,*
*the old man which grows corrupt*
*according to the deceitful lusts,*
*and be renewed in the spirit of your mind,*
*and that you put on the new man*
*which was created according to God,*
*in true righteousness and true holiness."*
*Ephesians 4:22-24*

Therefore, we were created in Christ Jesus to be who God
decided and said we would be; His children birthed in His
image, holiness and divine power!

## Our identity is based on who God says we are

There are many examples in the Scriptures where God declared a person's identity.

For example, when God created Adam and Eve He spoke their identity and purpose over them.

*"And God said, Let us make man in*
*our image, after our likeness:*
*and let them have dominion*
*over the fish of the sea,*
*and over the fowl of the air, and over the cattle,*
*and over all the earth, and over every*
*creeping thing that creeps upon the earth.*
*So God created man in his own image,*
*in the image of God created he him;*
*male and female created he them.*
*And God blessed them, and*
*God said unto them,*
*Be fruitful, and multiply, and replenish*
*(fill) the earth, and subdue it:*
*and have dominion over the fish of the*
*sea, and over the fowl of the air,*
*and over every living thing that*
*moves upon the earth."*
*Genesis 1:26-28*

At His baptism Jesus Christ was declared by His heavenly Father to be His "*beloved son in whom He was well pleased*".

*"When He had been baptised,*
*Jesus came up immediately from the water;*
*and behold, the heavens were opened to Him,*
*and He saw the Spirit of God descending*
*like a dove, and alighting upon Him:*
*And suddenly a voice came from heaven,*
*saying, This is My beloved Son,*
*in whom I am well pleased."*
*Matthew 3:16-17*

Peter was also defined by the word of Christ.

*"And Simon Peter answered and said,*
*You are the Christ, the Son of the living God.*
*Jesus answered and said to him,*
*Blessed are you, Simon Bar-Jonah,*
*for flesh and blood has not revealed this*
*to you, but My Father who is in heaven.*
*And I also say to you that you are Peter,*
*and on this rock I will build my church,*
*and the gates of hell shall not prevail against it.*
*And I will give you the keys of*
*the kingdom of heaven,*

*and whatever you bind on earth
will be bound in heaven,
and whatever you loose on earth
will be loosed in heaven."
Matthew 16:16-19*

Timothy was defined by the prophetic word of the apostle Paul. This confirms the utmost importance of pastors, leaders and parents speaking what God has already declared about every believer's image and purpose.

*"Don't neglect the gift that is in you,
which was given to you by prophecy,
with the laying on of the hands of the elders.
Be diligent in these things. Give
yourself wholly to them,
that your progress may be revealed to all."
1Timothy 4:14-15*

*"For this cause, I remind you that you
should stir up the gift of God
which is in you through the
laying on of my hands.
For God didn't give us a spirit of fear,
but of power, love, and self-control."
2Timothy 1:6-7*

## Knowing Jesus equals knowing ourselves

Like Peter's experience, when we know by revelation who Jesus Christ is we will know who we are! Our true identity and self-image is discovered in the revelation of Jesus Christ and who He declares us to be!

### We live out from who we are in Christ: God-like in nature, character, mind, heart, speech and action!

Our identity in Christ is a state of being - an accomplished fact. This new creation in Christ is a state of being. It presents the born again, born from above (heaven) child of God with the revelation, the knowledge and the confidence to '*just be*' in Christ.

> *"For in Him we live, and move, and have our being."*
> *Acts 17:28*

From this position the spiritual person is not trying to become or do, but rather lives in a present, continuous 'state of being' by seeing, thinking, speaking and acting out from his identity in Christ.

**Self-worth flows from our identity,
which is based on who God says we are;
I am who God says I am!**

**WHO I AM IN CHRIST
We are defined by who God
says we are in His Word**

*"That the sharing of your faith
may become effective by the acknowledging
of every good thing which is in you in Christ Jesus."
Philemon 1:6*

**Loved**: Jn. 3:16/ Eph. 5:1-2
**Called**: 1 Cor. 1:7-8 / I Pet. 2:21 / 2 Pet. 1:3
**Chosen**: 1 Pet. 2:9-10
**Forgiven**: 1 Pet. 2:24 / 1 Jn. 1:9
**Saved**: Eph. 2:4-10 / 2 Tim. 1:9
**Redeemed**: Eph. 1:6-8
**Made alive with Christ**: Eph 2:5
**Adopted**: Eph 1:5
**Righteous**: 2 Cor. 5:21 / Ps. 37:5-6
**Enriched**: 1 Cor. 1:4-5
**Sanctified**: 1 Thess. 5:23
**Washed clean**: Ps. 51:7 / Is. 1:18
**Justified**: Rom 8:28-30 / Rom 5:1
**Given Christ's Spirit**: 2 Tim. 1:7

**Sealed by Christ's Spirit**: Eph 1:13
**Led by the Spirit of God**: Rom 8:14
**Anointed**: 1 Jn. 2:27 / Ps 20:6, 23:5
**Raised and Seated with Christ**: Eph 2:6
**Made New**: 2 Cor. 5:17 / Eph. 4:22
**Given Eternal Life**: Jn 3:16
**Being Conformed to the image of Christ**: Rom 8:29
**Accepted in Christ**: Eph 1:6
**Given Revelation**: Eph 1:9,17-18 / 1Cor 2:9-12
**A child of God**: Gal. 4:7 / Jn. 1:12
**Co-heir with Christ**: Rom. 8:15-17
**Seated with Christ**: Eph. 2:6
**Ambassador**: 2 Cor. 5:20
**A Living Stone**: 1 Pet. 2:5
**Christ's friend**: Jn. 15:15
**A temple of God**: 1 Cor 6:19
**Crucified with Christ**: Gal 2:20
**Given Spiritual Authority**: Luke 10:19
**A member of Christ's Body**: 1 Cor. 12:27
**Equipped**: Eph. 4:11-13, 6:10-19 / 2 Tim. 3:16-17
**Protected**: Ps. 9 / Ps. 34:7
**Victorious**: 1 Jn. 5:4
**Free**: Gal. 5:1
**Filled and Complete**: Col. 1:9-14, 2:9-10
**Healed**:  1 Pet. 2:24-25 / Is. 53.5
**Blessed**: Eph. 1:3

**Have peace**: Phil. 4:4-9
**Comforted**: Ps. 34:17-18 / 119:76
**Hopeful**: Heb. 6:19, 10:23, 1 Pet. 1:3
**Bold Access**: Heb 4:14-16 / Eph. 3:12
**Beloved**: Jer. 31:3 / Col. 3:12
**Free from Condemnation**: Rom 8:1
**Holy and Blameless**: Eph 1:4 / Col. 1:22
**Called to be Salt and Light**: Mt. 5:13-14
**Brought near**: Eph. 2:13
**Strong**: Phil. 4:13 / Eph. 6:10
**Prospered**: 3Jn 2Phil. 4:19 / Mt. 6:33
**Rested**: Ps. 62.1 / Mt. 11.28-29
**Pleasing to God**: Rom 8:8-9
**Christ's Workmanship:** Eph. 2:10
**Chosen fruit bearer**: Jn. 15:16
**Joyful**: Ps. 34.5
**Reconciled to Christ**: 2 Cor. 5:18-19
**A Child of Light**: 1 Thess. 5:5
**Hidden in Christ**: Col 3:3
**Never Alone**: Deut. 31:8 / Heb 13:5
**Never disappointed**: Rom 10:11
**A Saint of God**: Eph 4:12 / Eph 2:19

> *"For in Him dwells all the fulness*
> *of the Godhead bodily.*
> *And you are complete in Him."*
> *Colossians 2:9-10*

## Chapter Six

# THE CREATIVE POWER OF OUR WORDS

There is power in words. From the very beginning we see God creating everything through His divine, powerful and creative words.

> *"Through faith we understand that the worlds were framed by the word of God, so that things which are seen were not made of things which were visible."*
> *Hebrews 11:3*

From the beginning we also see the devil seeking to counter the Word of God, not with creativity but with destruction. Nothing has changed!

And so it is with us. We are called by God to align ourselves with His Word.

This alignment with the Word of God is dependent on two things:-

1. What we're thinking in our **hearts**

2. What we're speaking out of our **mouths**

The church is built in a climate of war. We are in this spiritual war because we have joined God's side and the devil is trying to counter the Word of God with his words.

*"For though we walk in the flesh,*
*we do not war after the flesh:*
*For the weapons of our warfare are not carnal,*
*but mighty through God to the*
*pulling down of strong holds;)*
*Casting down imaginations,*
*and every high thing that exalts itself*
*against the knowledge of God,*
*and bringing into captivity every thought*
*to the obedience of Christ."*
*2Corinthians 10:3-5*

## God does everything through words

God does everything through words: His divine words, creative words, loving words, redeeming words and empowering words.

Therefore, the chief weapon of the devil is words to counter God's words.

However, the devil has nothing to counter God with any effect because he is defeated. He has no authority.

The devil is "*disarmed*" and rendered powerless and impotent before God. The Lord Jesus Christ defeated the devil and rendered him powerless through His death and resurrection. Jesus has won!

> *"Having wiped out the handwriting of*
> *requirements that was against us,*
> *which was contrary to us. And He*
> *has taken it out of the way,*
> *having nailed it to the cross;*
> *Having disarmed principalities and powers,*
> *He made a public spectacle of them,*
> *triumphing over them in it."*
> *Colossians 2:14-15*

## The Devil works through lying, counter words

But the devil has found a cunning and deceitful way to cause trouble and disrupt the work of God. He uses counter words, deceiving words, divisive words, lying words and words that destroy, disrupt and sabotage. This is the way the devil has worked from the very beginning.

*"Why do you not understand my speech?*
*even because you cannot hear my word.*
*You are of your father the devil and*
*the lusts of your father you will do.*
*He was a murderer from the beginning,*
*and abode not in the truth,*
*because there is no truth in him.*
*When he speaks a lie, he speaks of his own:*
*for he is a liar, and the father of it."*
*John 8:43-44*

Because the Devil has been rendered impotent before Christ his only method is to undermine God's Word. We see this at the very beginning at the temptation of Adam and Eve.

The devil used a progressive and yet plausible use of words to deceive them.

The devil:-

1. **Questioned the Word of God** - "*Has God Said?" (Genesis 3:1)*
2. Then, **denied the Word of God** - **"***Surely you will not die" (Genesis 3:4)*
3. And finally, **replaced the Word of God** - **"***For God knows...you will be like God" (Genesis 3:5 Amplified Bible)*

**The ultimate goal of the devil
is to replace God's Word with his word**

When we understand this we can identify the atmospheres, circumstances, situations and the people that the devil is using to 'talk to us'. They can have a message from the devil in what they do and in what they say!

**Negative Vs Positive dialogue**

The tendency that exists in all of us as humans is to listen to the 'dialogue of negativity' around us, instead of listening to 'dialogue of positivity' in God and His Word.

**When I repeat the message
that the devil is speaking,**

## I accept the atmosphere that he is trying to create!

When we are with negative people and we adopt 'their message' of complaining, criticism, cynicism, fear and doubt, we also accept their atmosphere that they are creating for themselves through their words.

## God's atmosphere flows through God's Word

God's atmosphere flows into our lives when we release the Word of God that is in our hearts through the words of our mouth!

> *"I assure you: If anyone **SAYS** to this mountain,*
> *'Be lifted up and thrown into the sea,'*
> *and does not doubt  in his **HEART**,*
> *but believes that what he **SAYS** will happen,*
> *it will be done for him."*
> *Mark 11:23*

## There is a direct connection between what is in our hearts and mouths and what we are experiencing in our lives

## The Word of God is the kingdom of God language

The Word of God is the kingdom way of thinking and speaking. The Word of God is the '*normal Christian*' language.

The Bible begins in Genesis with God speaking things into being from the void, from the nothing, from the chaos.

God is proactive and always at work. He is hovering over things that have no shape; the chaos, the void and the darkness.

God sees things that are not working properly, that don't seem to have any future in them. Then God begins to speak to those void, empty, chaotic and dark things like He did on creation day.

*"In the beginning God created
the heaven and the earth.
And the earth was without form, and void;
and darkness was upon the face of the deep.
And the Spirit of God moved
upon the face of the waters.
And God said, Let there be light:
and there was light."
Genesis 1:1-3*

## God works through the spoken word

Why do the Scriptures constantly present God speaking to create? Did He record this for His own benefit?

Not at all!

God is demonstrating and exemplifying His way of doing things to His children. God works through His spoken word and calls us to be like Him; "*calling the things that be not as though they were*".

> *"God, who gives life to the dead*
> *and calls those things which do not*
> *exist as though they did."*
> *Romans 4:17*

## God calls us to speak and change things through His Word by faith

God wants us to speak by faith to situations, atmospheres and problems in our lives to bring about kingdom change and create kingdom atmospheres. This is how our lives, our marriages, our families, our churches and our world will begin to be like God's Word says they should be!

The way to change something God's way is not by fighting it, not by getting mad at it, not by freezing up with fear, or by working harder.

Change happens by speaking God's Word in faith to it; changing things God's way!

When God looks at something He doesn't like, He doesn't back off, accept it or feel defeated. He starts speaking to it. He speaks to it the way He wants it to be!

It doesn't have a choice, it doesn't argue with Him, it doesn't come back at Him, it must become what He has said it is to be! God's Word is omnipotent!

On creation morning when God commanded, *"Let there be light", the* darkness didn't say, "I'll think about it!" Or, "Hey God, I like being dark, go away!" The dark had to become what God said it had to be: LIGHT!

When the devil attacks us we can feel like the victim and begin to complain and accept defeat. We stop speaking faith. We stop speaking God's Word into our situation and begin to speak the Devil's word about it.

However, God has created us to believe, speak and act like Him!

God is sending us into the world to make a difference. We are called by God to live with a new mindset, a kingdom mindset.

### We are sent by God to make a difference

When we turn up the kingdom of God turns up, because the kingdom of God is within us!

> *"Neither shall they say, Lo here! or, lo there!*
> *for, behold, **the kingdom of***
> ***God is within you.***"
> *Luke 17:21*

We are sent by God into the world to create a new order, to bring about kingdom change and to make a difference through our words.

There is power in our words to create change and to make a difference, especially when we speak God's Word!

The key is to begin speaking the living, active Word of God now, today, into our world and into our circumstances.

Then we will see how God can transform the darkness, the void and the chaos around us into love, joy and peace.

**Your circumstances and atmospheres
weren't designed to influence
and change you,
You were designed to influence
and change them,
by speaking the eternal, transforming
power of the Word of God!**

*"So shall My word be that goes
forth from My mouth;
It shall not return to Me void,
But it shall accomplish what I please,
And it shall prosper in the thing
for which I sent it."
Isaiah 55:11*

## Chapter Seven

# LIVING IN FREEDOM

*"Now the Lord is the Spirit, and
where the Spirit of the Lord is,
**THERE IS FREEDOM.**"*
*2Corinthians 3:17*

I remember when I was young, doing some off-shore net fishing with a friend when he got into trouble. What I didn't realise until later was that he couldn't swim! So I sprang into action pulling him out or the dangerous rip to safety.

When his wife heard the story she made me a cake in the shape of a lifesaver lolly and presented it to me the next day. She declared to everyone present that I was my friend's and her "lifesaver", a hero!

Of course, I found this quite overwhelming because I only did the right thing for my friend who was in trouble.

However, she went on to announce that they would be forever indebted to me because of what I did in saving her husband's life.

## Debtors to Christ

How much more are we indebted and obligated to the Lord Jesus Christ to live our lives for Him!

*"For the love of Christ compels us;*
*because we judge thus;*
*that if One died for all, then all died;*
*And He died for all, that those who live*
*should live no longer for themselves,*
*but for Him who died for them and rose again."*
*2Corinthians 5:14-15*

This is because He paid the ultimate price and sacrifice by laying down His life for us!

*"So then, brothers and sisters,*
***we are under obligation***,
*not to the flesh, to live according to the flesh*
*(for if you live according to*
*the flesh, you will die),*
*but if by the Spirit you put to death the*

*deeds of the body you will live.*
*For all who are led by the Spirit of*
*God are the sons of God."*
*Romans 8:12-14 NET*

On the cross the Lord Jesus Christ set us free from the wages and the power of sin and death, so how can we withhold anything from Him?

## "IF JESUS CHRIST BE GOD
## AND DIED FOR ME,
## THEN NO SACRIFICE CAN BE TOO GREAT
## FOR ME TO MAKE FOR HIM"
## CT Studd

### Slaves of sin to servants of God

*"Being then made free from sin, you*
*became the servants of righteousness.*
*I speak after the manner of men because*
*of the infirmity of your flesh:*
*for as you have yielded your members*
*servants to uncleanness*
*and to iniquity to iniquity;*
*even so now yield your members servants*
*to righteousness unto holiness.*

*For when you were the servants of sin,*
*you were free from righteousness.*
*But now being made free from sin,*
*and become servants to God,*
*you have your fruit unto holiness,*
*and the end everlasting life."*
*Romans 6:18-22*

## The new spiritual law - *"The Law of the Spirit of Life in Christ Jesus"*

Through His death, burial and resurrection Jesus Christ set us free from sin and death, the flesh and the Devil and established a new spiritual law: "**the Law of the Spirit of Life**".

This replaced the old law of "*the Law of Sin and Death*" and set us free from all the requirements and punishments of the law.

*"For the law of the spirit of life in Christ Jesus*
*has made me free from the*
*law of sin and death."*
*Romans 8:2*

Before Christ came we were all subjected to this "*law of sin and death*", because the law declared that we were all sinners. We have all sinned and therefore we must pay the penalty of death for our sins.

> "*For all have sinned, and fall*
> *short of the glory of God."*
> *Romans 3:23*

> "*For the wages of sin is death;*
> *but the gift of God is eternal life*
> *through Jesus Christ our Lord."*
> *Romans 6:23*

When Jesus went to the cross He not only paid for the penalty of our sins through His death. He also rose again by the power of the Spirit of God to give us a new life through the establishing of a new law – the "**law of the Spirit of life**".

The provision and experience of the new birth transfers us from the "*law of sin and death*" to the "*law of the spirit of life*" in Christ Jesus. We are set free from sin and death to serve Christ.

## The old law is fulfilled and superseded by the new law

This new law of Christ frees us from the old law and the commandments because it fulfils and supersedes the law through the divine power of His cross and resurrection.

> *"But now we are delivered from the law,*
> *that being dead wherein we were held;*
> *that we should serve in newness of spirit,*
> *and not in the oldness of the letter."*
> *Romans 7:6*

## We can't live by the law and grace at the same time

Imagine immigrants coming to a free, democratic country like Australia or the USA, but continue to live in fear and subjugation to the old laws of their former country. They might be set free from the physical environment of their former country, but they are not living free lives in their new country.

The same is true in God's kingdom. We can't live under the old law of works and the new law of faith at the same time because they are **two totally different systems**. They are diametrically opposed to each other!

*"What shall we say then?*
*Shall we continue in sin, that grace may abound?*
*Certainly not! How shall we who died*
*to sin live any longer in it?"*
*Romans 6:1-2*

The Lord Jesus Christ has freed us from the law so we can live for Him "*under grace*" by faith!

*"For sin shall not have dominion over you:*
*for you are not under the law, but under grace."*
*Romans 6:14*

## The natural is superseded by the spiritual

The old law of works is 'natural' which works through human effort, while the new law of Christ is 'spiritual' which works through faith in the endless, resurrection life and power of Christ.

*"Who has come, not according to the*
*law of a fleshly commandment;*
*but according to the power of an endless life.*
*For he testifies: You are a priest forever*
*according the order of Melchizedek."*
*Hebrew 7:16-17*

Because the old law of works relied on the flesh, or natural effort, it was weakened and resulted in failure.

Therefore, the old law was unable to perfect those who served in it because it was based on imperfect sacrifices.

*"For on one hand there is an annulling*
*of the former commandment*
*because of its weakness and unprofitableness."*
*Hebrews 7:18*

## The new law of Christ produced perfection: a superior new covenant

In contrast, the new law of Christ was established on the perfect sacrifice of the Lord Jesus Christ so it made those forgiven perfect in the sight of God!

*For the law made nothing perfect;*
*on the other hand, there is the*
*bringing in of a better hope,*
*through which we draw near to God."*
*Hebrews 7:19*

*"For by one offering He has perfected*
*forever those who are being sanctified."*
*Hebrews 10:14*

This makes the new covenant and the high priestly ministry of the Lord Jesus Christ superior and *"more excellent"* in every way!

> *"But now He has obtained a*
> *more excellent ministry,*
> *inasmuch as He is also Mediator*
> *of a better covenant,*
> *which was established on better promises."*
> *Hebrews 8:6*

Therefore, to live by the natural law of works means we are doomed for failure because it is a powerless endeavour of human effort. The focus of living by works is to keep the law as best we can, even though we know that we can never succeed in meeting the law's requirements.

The new law of Christ, however, is spiritual and supernatural, imparting life and power to the believer to be victorious over sin. The focus of living by faith is to please the Lord Jesus Christ through living by the Holy Spirit's power and guidance.

## The normal Christian lives fulfilling the law

This supernatural new life in Christ results in the normal Christian fulfilling, or superseding, the law by Christ's empowering grace and life!

*"For what the law could not do,*
*in that it was weak through the flesh,*
*God sending his own Son in the*
*likeness of sinful flesh, and for sin,*
*condemned sin in the flesh:*
*That the righteousness of the law*
*might be fulfilled in us,*
*who walk not after the flesh, but after the Spirit."*
*Romans 8:3-4*

## The perfect sacrifice of Christ removes the consciousness of sin

Because the perfect sacrifice of Christ removes sin forever, it is normal for the spiritual person to live more conscious of righteousness than sin!

*"For then would they not have*
*ceased to be offered?*
*because that the worshippers once purged*

> *should have had no more conscience of sins.*
> *But in those sacrifices there is a remembrance*
> *again made of sins every year."*
> *Hebrews 10:2-3*

## Set free from the power of sin

We no longer live conscious of sin because we are free from the power and influence of sin in our lives.

We no longer live to obey a law that will save us because we are already saved and set free by Christ from the law and religious works.

We no longer live in fear that the penalty of death awaits us because Christ has set us free from the penalty of sin. Therefore the bondage of the fear of death is removed!

> *"Forasmuch then as the children are*
> *partakers of flesh and blood,*
> *he also himself likewise took part of the same;*
> *that through death he might destroy him that*
> *had the power of death, that is, the devil;*
> *And deliver them who through fear of death*
> *were all their lifetime subject to bondage."*
> *Hebrews 2:14-15*

We now live in faith, hope and love. We are free indeed!

*"Therefore, if the Son makes you free,*
*you shall be free indeed!"*
*John 8:36*

*"For freedom Christ has set us free;*
*Stand firm therefore,*
*And do not submit again to a yoke of slavery."*
*Galatians 5:1*

## THE CHALLENGE FOR ALL CHRISTIANS IS NOT TO BEGIN FREE - THAT'S A GIFT FROM GOD THE CHALLENGE IS TO CONTINUE TO BE FREE THROUGH LIVING BY FAITH

*"You were running well.*
*Who hindered you from obeying the truth?"*
*Galatians 5:7*

### How to continue to live in freedom

The Scriptures outline the following 5 ways to continue to live in freedom.

## 1. Live out from Your Spirit

> *"For if I pray in a tongue, my spirit prays..."*
> *1Corinthians 14:14*

> *"For he who speaks in a tongue*
> *speaks not to men but to God;*
> *for no one understands him,*
> *but he **UTTERS MYSTERIES IN THE SPIRIT**."*
> *1Corinthians 14:2*

That is, living out from our spirit, or inner being, is about adopting a '**Spiritual Orientation and Mindset**' by faith.

> *"For those who live according to the flesh*
> *set their minds on the things of the flesh,*
> *but those who live according to the Spirit,*
> *the things of the Spirit.*
> *For the mind of the flesh is death,*
> *but the mind of the Spirit is life and peace;*
> *because the mind of the flesh*
> *is hostile towards God;*
> *for it is not subject to God's law,*
> *neither indeed can it be.*
> *Those who are in the flesh can't please God.*
> *But you are not in the flesh but in the Spirit,*
> *If it is so that the Spirit of God dwells in you."*
> *Rom 8:5-9 (WEB)*

## 2. Keep your spirit clear and free from sin, unbelief and offences

There is a constant, daily need for vigilance in keeping our hearts pure before God; untainted by sin, unbelief and offences.

*"Having therefore these
promises, dearly beloved,
let us cleanse ourselves from all
filthiness of the flesh and spirit,
perfecting holiness in the fear of God."
2Corinthians 7:1*

*"Keep your heart with all diligence; for
out of it are (flow) the issues of life."
Proverbs 4:23*

*"Guard your heart with all vigilance,
for from it are the sources of life."
(NET Bible)*

*"...out of it is the wellspring of life."
(World English Bible)*

## 3. Operate in the Discernment of the Holy Spirit

To keep free in Christ requires an attitude of spiritual discernment, especially in the environment in which we live in today. It is important to be clear in our minds as to what the Holy Spirit is revealing to us and leading us into.

*"But God has revealed them to us by His Spirit:*
*For the Spirit searches all things, yes,*
*The deep things of God."*
*1Cor 2:10*

## 4. Walk in the Spirit

Once we know what God is saying to us in His Word and revealing to us through the Holy Spirit, it is important to walk in those things with confidence and conviction.

*"Now the works of the flesh are evident:*
*sexual immorality, impurity,*
*sensuality, idolatry, sorcery,*
*enmity, strife, jealousy, fits of*
*anger, rivalries, dissensions,*
*divisions, envy, drunkenness,*
*orgies and things like these.*
*I warn you, as I warned you before,*
*that those who Do such things will*

*not inherit the kingdom of God.*
*But the fruit of the Spirit is love, joy, peace,*
*patience, kindness, goodness,*
*faithfulness, gentleness, self-control;*
*against such things there is no law."*
*Galatians 5:19-23*

*"If we live in the Spirit, Let us*
*also walk in the Spirit."*
*Galatians 5:25*

## 5. Serve Others Unconditionally Through Love

*"Paul, a bondservant of Jesus Christ."*
*Romans 1:1*

The apostle Paul uses the word "*slave*" ("*bondservant*") which is "*doulas*" (G1401) meaning "*someone who belongs to another, without any ownership rights of their own*".

This indicates that he was freely and willingly bound for life as a slave of Christ to serve Him as a 'love slave'. His idea is not one of tyranny and servitude from fear and torment, but rather one of a willing response of love to love.

This is all because of Christ's eternal and unselfish love in giving up all to redeem and purchase our salvation.

## FROM SLAVES OF FEAR
## TO SLAVES OF LOVE

*"For you were bought with a price:*
*therefore glorify God in your*
*body, and in your spirit,*
*which are God's."*
*1 Corinthians 6:20*

*"You were bought with a price:*
*don't be the servants of men."*
*1 Corinthians 7:23*

## WE WERE BOUGHT WITH A PRICE
## THEREFORE OUR NATURAL RESPONSE
## IS TO BE BOUND BY LOVE FOR LIFE
## TO OUR LORD AND SAVIOUR JESUS CHRIST

## THIS IS TRUE FREEDOM!

By being Christ's 'love slave' we are totally under His benevolent blessing, protection and care and we are no longer burdened down with the *"cares of this life"*.

We are truly free and no longer serve ourselves or men. Now we unconditionally serve our Lord and Saviour Jesus Christ.

## From slavery of tyranny to service of friendship and love

In the movie "*The Eagle*", a Celtic slave called Esca hated his Roman master but was saved from death by his master.

This story shows how his relationship with his master changed from a slavery of tyranny, fear and hatred to a service of friendship and love.

This is the idea that Paul is using to illustrate for us in Romans and Galatians. Because of sin we were bound in a slavery of tyranny to the devil. But through Jesus Christ we have been set free in order to enter into a service of friendship and love.

> *"You were called to freedom, brothers.*
> *Only do not use your freedom as*
> *an opportunity for the flesh,*
> *But through love serve one another."*
> *Galatians 5:13*

## Serving others keeps us free

Serving others keeps our freedom positive, outward, contextualised. When we use our freedom for our own selfish desires we will end up complicating life and bringing ourselves back into bondage.

The writer to the Hebrews sums up this perfect, free life in describing the normal lifestyle of the spiritual person:-

*"Having therefore, brethren,*
*boldness to enter into the holiest*
*by the blood of Jesus,*
*By a new and living way, which*
*he hath consecrated for us,*
*through the veil, that is to say, his flesh;*
*And having an high priest over*
*the house of God;*
*Let us draw near with a true heart*
*in full assurance of faith,*
*having our hearts sprinkled*
*from an evil conscience,*
*and our bodies washed with pure water.*
*Let us hold fast the profession of*
*our faith without wavering;*
*(for he is faithful that promised;)*
*And let us consider one another to*

*provoke unto love and to good works:*
*Not forsaking the assembling of ourselves*
*together, as the manner of some is;*
*but exhorting one another:*
*and so much the more, as ye see*
*the day approaching."*
*Hebrews 10:19-25*

The normal Christian has:

* Boldness
* Entrance into the holiest
* A new and living way
* Connection to our High Priest
* Possession of full assurance of faith
* A pure heart and conscience
* The profession of faith
* Consideration of others
* The habitual assembling together with the church
* Encourages others
* Sees the coming Day of the Lord

## Chapter Eight

# LIVING IN DIVINE HEALTH SPIRITUALLY

*"Beloved, I pray that you may prosper
in all things and be in health,
just as your soul prospers."*
3John 2

*"Dear friend, I pray that you
may prosper in every way
and be in good health physically
just as you are spiritually."*
3John 2 HCSB

The Lord Jesus Christ accomplished the **forgiveness** of our sins and the **healing** of our bodies on the cross.

*"He took our **infirmities** and*
*bore our **sicknesses**."*
*Matthew 8:17*

*Who Himself bore our **sins** in*
*His own body on a tree...*
*by whose stripes you were **healed**."*
*1Peter 2:24*

The word "*bore*" is from an Old Testament word referring to the Scapegoat on the Day of Atonement, which carried away the sins of the children of Israel into the wilderness.

This was a picture foreshadowing the sacrifice of Christ in which He would carry our sins away from us.

*"But the goat, on which the lot*
*fell to be the scapegoat,*
*shall be presented alive before the Lord,*
*to make an atonement with him,*
*and to let him go for a scapegoat*
*into the wilderness."*
*Leviticus 16:10*

*"And Aaron shall lay both his hands*
*upon the head of the live goat,*
*and confess over him all the iniquities*

> *of the children of Israel,*
> *and all their transgressions in all their sins,*
> *putting them upon the head of the goat,*
> *and shall send him away by the hand*
> *of a fit man into the wilderness:*
> *And the goat shall bear upon him all their*
> *iniquities to a land not inhabited:*
> *and he shall let go the goat in the wilderness."*
> *Leviticus 16:21-22*

Jesus Christ is our *'scapegoat'* who "*bore*" our sins and sicknesses so we could live in divine health spiritually and physically.

We are now "*complete in Christ*" who has provided full and complete salvation for us through His cross.

> *"For in Him dwells all the fullness*
> *of the Godhead bodily;*
> *and you are complete in Him."*
> *Colossians 2:10*

Complete provision for everything we need has been made at the cross of Christ.

> *"His divine power has **given us all things***
> *that pertain to **life** (physical and*

*material) and **godliness** (spiritual)..."*
*2Peter 1:3*

## Faith in the provisions of Christ at the cross

Our faith is in the fact that sin and sickness stopped at the cross where we were forgiven, cleansed and justified and by the Lord Jesus Christ.

*"Who his own self **bore our sins***
*in His own body on the tree,*
*that we, being dead to sins, should*
*live unto righteousness:*
*by whose stripes you were healed."*
*1Peter 2:24*

Faith in Christ accepts His perfect and complete provision on the cross as an accomplished fact.

Therefore, faith declares that, "If we **were** forgiven and healed at the cross, then we **are** forgiven and healed now!"

## Jesus Christ destroyed the power of sin at the cross

Sin and its power was destroyed at the cross through the substitutionary death of Jesus Christ for us. Therefore, through faith in Christ we also die to sin and its power over our lives.

> *"Shall we continue in sin that*
> *grace may abound?*
> *Certainly not!*
> *How shall we who died to sin*
> *live any longer in it?"*
> *Romans 6:1-2*

## We are now set free from sin: 'sin-free'

> *"For he who has died*
> *has been **freed from sin.**"*
> *Romans 6:7*

Through faith we are raised with Christ to live a '**sin-free life**': **a life free from the power, influence and effects of sin over our lives!**

> *"whoever has been born of God does not sin,*
> *for His seed remains in him;*
> *and he cannot sin because he*
> *has been born of God."*
> *1John 3:9*

## 'Sinless' or 'Sin free'

What is the difference between being '**sinless**' and being '**sin-free**'?

'**Sinless**' means that we never, ever sin because we have been made perfect by Christ. However, we are not made perfect in this life, only powerful!

### Not perfect in this life, only powerful!

Cults and man-made religions present and demand the idea that a Christian must be '**sinless**' and issue penalties for those who fail.

> *"If we say that we have no sin,*
> *we deceive ourselves,*
> *and the truth is not in us."*
> *1John 1:8*

However, the Scriptures teach us that we will be made 'sinless' and "*incorruptible*" at the coming of Christ when we experience the resurrection of our bodies by the power of Christ!

> *"So also is the resurrection of the dead.*
> *It is sown in corruption; it is*

> *raised in incorruption:*
> *It is sown in dishonour; it is raised in glory:*
> *it is sown in weakness; it is raised in power:*
> *It is sown a natural body; it is*
> *raised a spiritual body.*
> *There is a natural body, and*
> *there is a spiritual body.*
> *And so it is written, The first man*
> *Adam was made a living soul;*
> *the last Adam was made a quickening spirit."*
> *1Corinthians 15:42-45*

## Sin and temptation are ever present in this life

The fact remains that sin and temptation and the possibility of sinning are ever present in this life. This is why the Scriptures constantly encourage us to be vigilant and discerning.

> *"Therefore let him who thinks he*
> *stands take heed lest he fall."*
> *1Corinthians 10:12*

In Christ we are empowered *"to escape"* and *"endure"* temptation and to live free of sin and all it's devastating effects.

*"No temptation has taken you*
*except what is common to man.*
*God is faithful, who will not allow you to*
*be tempted above what you are able,*
*but will with the temptation also*
*make the way of escape,*
*that you may be able to endure it."*
*1Corinthians 10:13 WEB*

## Living in victory over our sinful nature

In this life we live with two natures: the *"flesh"* (the *"old man"*) and the *"spirit"* (the *"new man")*.

The '*normal Christian*' has been united with Christ and is set free from the slavery of the *"flesh"* and *"sin"* and lives empowered by the Holy Spirit.

*"Knowing this, that our old man*
*was crucified with Him,*
*that the body of sin might be done away with,*
*that we should no longer be slaves of sin."*
*Romans 6:6*

The '*normal Christian*' has a new focus and orientation to live *"according to the Spirit"* and not *"according to the flesh"*.

> *"For those who live according to the flesh*
> *set their minds on the things of the flesh,*
> *but those who live according to the*
> *Spirit, the things of the Spirit*
> *"For to be carnally minded is death,*
> *but to be spiritually minded is life and peace."*
> *Romans 8:5-6*

So what happens "**IF**" we do sin?

> *"And **IF** anyone sins,*
> *we have an advocate with the Father,*
> *Jesus Christ the righteous."*
> *1John 2:1*

It is important to notice the use of the word "**IF**", not '**WHEN**', by the apostle John.

We weren't born again supernaturally to sin, to fail or to do wrong. Rather, we were born again to be righteous, holy, to overcome and to do right!

> *"Therefore do not let sin reign*
> *in your mortal body,*
> *that you should obey it in it's lusts.*
> *And do not present your members as*
> *instruments of unrighteousness to sin,*

*but present yourselves to God as
being alive from the dead,
and your members as instruments
of righteousness to God.
For sin shall not have dominion over you,
for you are not under law but under grace."
Romans 6:12-14*

## The Example of boats - designed to float

If I was buying a boat and the seller told me the reason they were selling was because their boat was designed to sink! Would I buy that boat? No, I wouldn't! Because boats aren't designed to sink, they're designed to float!

So, if boats are designed to float why is there a need for lifeboats and life jackets?

These life saving devices are on every boat not for '**WHEN'** it sinks, but '**IF'** it sinks!

They are on board as an emergency provision so that '**IF**' extraordinary and rare circumstances occur that causes the boat to sink provision has already been made to save the lives on board.

This is exactly the same in dealing with sin. The normal Christian has been forgiven, cleansed and set free from sin; Jesus Christ our "*saviour*".

However, Jesus Christ is also our "*advocate*", or 'lifeboat', so that "**IF**" extraordinary and rare circumstances occur that we do sin provision has already been made to save our lives from sin!

> *"If we confess our sins, he is faithful*
> *and just to forgive us our sins,*
> *and to cleanse us from all unrighteousness."*
> *1John 1:9*

In other words, we have been born again by the power of the Holy Spirit to live a 'sin free' life of spiritual health in Christ!

> *"For whatever is born of God*
> *overcomes the world,*
> *and this is the victory that overcomes the world*
> *- our faith."*
> *1John 5:4*

## Chapter Nine

# LIVING IN DIVINE PROSPERITY AND SUPPLY

*"Beloved, I pray that you may
prosper in all things
and be in health, just as your soul prospers."
3John 2*

*"For you know the grace of
our Lord Jesus Christ,
that, though He was rich, yet for
your sakes He became poor,
that you through His poverty might be rich."
2Corinthians 8:9*

## Defining Biblical prosperity

It is important to define Biblical prosperity because there is so much misunderstanding about what prosperity is from God's perspective.

Some Christians believe that poverty is a sign of true spirituality and God's blessing on their lives! However, the Scriptures continually present God as our kind and generous heavenly Father who showers His manifold blessings upon all His children.

> *"He that spared not His own Son,*
> *but delivered Him up for us all,*
> *how shall He not with Him also*
> *freely give us all things?"*
> *Romans 8:32*

## God is magnanimous, benevolent and generous: the perfect gift giver

To understand 'divine prosperity' we must first understand the nature of God. It is God's nature to bless and to prosper His children because He is kind, benevolent, generous and magnanimous. It is God's nature to bless and to give!

*"For the Lord God is a sun and shield:*
*the Lord will give grace and glory:*
*no good thing will He withhold*
*from them who walk uprightly.*
*O Lord of hosts, blessed is the*
*man that trusts in You."*
*Psalm 84:11-12*

God's intention in Christ is to enrich our lives in everything…
spiritually, emotionally, mentally, physically and financially.

*"The blessing of the Lord, it makes rich,*
*and he adds no sorrow with it."*
*Proverbs 10:22*

*"Every good gift and every*
*perfect gift is from above,*
*and comes down from the Father of lights,*
*with whom is no variableness,*
*neither shadow of turning."*
*James 1:17*

## God's blessings are never restricted to the spiritual

To hold the view that God's redeeming provisions in the
New Covenant are restricted to the spiritual is inconsistent

with the Scriptures. This would reduce the provision of Christ's new covenant to be less than the provisions of the old covenant.

In fact, Christ has excelled way above and beyond the old covenant with a "*more excellent*" and "*better*" new covenant; "*more excellent ministry, a better covenant and better promises*"!

> "*But now He has obtained a*
> **more excellent ministry**,
> *by how much also He is the mediator*
> *of a* **better covenant**,
> *which was established upon* **better promises**."
> *Hebrews 8:6*

There is no restriction or limitation on the blessings of God because Christ's provisions at the cross were full and complete providing us with "**all (every) spiritual blessing**"!

> "*Blessed be the God and Father*
> *of our Lord Jesus Christ,*
> *who has blessed us with all (every) spiritual*
> *blessing in heavenly places in Christ.*"
> *Ephesians 1:3*

King David understood that the blessings and benefits of the Lord effected every area of our lives:-

*"Bless the Lord, O my soul:*
*and all that is within me, bless His holy name.*
*Bless the Lord, O my soul, and*
*forget not all His benefits,*
*Who forgives all your iniquities;*
*who heals all your diseases;*
*Who redeems your life from destruction;*
*who crowns you with lovingkindness*
*and tender mercies;*
*Who satisfies your mouth with good things;*
*so that your youth is renewed like the eagle's."*
*Psalm 103:1-5*

* forgiveness of sin
* healing of our physical bodies
* redemption from destruction
* crowning our lives with loving kindness and tender mercies
* provision and blessing on our food
* blessing us with youthful vigour

Also, God's blessings are not restricted to those who love Him.

*"But I say to you, Love your enemies,*
*bless them that curse you, do*
*good to them that hate you,*
*and pray for them who despitefully*
*use you, and persecute you;*
*That you may be the children of*
*your Father who is in heaven:*
*for He makes His sun to rise on*
*the evil and on the good,*
*and sends rain on the just and on the unjust."*
*Matthew 5:44-45*

## God's blessings of Prosperity through the Scriptures

## Abraham was prospered by God

All God's people from antiquity were prospered by God. Chiefly, our *"father of faith Abraham" was greatly prospered by God.*

*"And Abram was **very rich** in*
*cattle, in silver, and in gold."*
*Genesis 13:2*

*"And Abraham was old, and well stricken in age:*
*and the Lord had **blessed***

**Abraham in all things**...
*And the Lord has blessed my master
greatly; and he is become great:
and He has given him flocks, and
herds, and silver, and gold,
and menservants, and maidservants,
and camels, and asses."
Genesis 24:1, 35*

## Isaac was greatly prospered by God

*"Then Isaac sowed in that land,
and received in the same year an hundredfold:
and the LORD blessed him.
And the man waxed great, and went forward,
and grew until he became very great."
For he had possession of flocks,
and possession of herds,
and great store of servants: and
the Philistines envied him."
Genesis 26:12-14*

## The Children of Israel were given power to "get", "make" and create wealth

*"But you shall remember the Lord your God:
for it is He that gives you **power to get wealth**,
that He may establish His covenant
which He swore to your fathers,
as it is this day."*
*Deuteronomy 8:18*

*"But you shall remember [with profound
respect] the LORD your God,
for it is He who is **giving you
power to make wealth**,
that He may confirm His covenant
which He swore (solemnly promised)
to your fathers, as it is this day."*
Amplified Bible

## The blessing of the upright is wealth and riches

*"Praise the Lord.
Blessed is the man that fears the Lord,
that delights greatly in His commandments.
His seed shall be mighty upon earth:
the generation of the upright shall be blessed.*

***Wealth and riches shall be in his house:***
*and his righteousness endures for ever."*
*Psalm 112:1-3*

## The blessing of Wisdom from God brings prosperity

*"Length of days is in her right hand;*
*and in her left hand **riches and honour**."*
*Proverbs 3:16*

## Honouring the Lord with our wealth increases prosperity

*"Honour the Lord with your substance,*
*and with the first fruits of all your **increase**:*
*So your barns will be filled with **plenty**,*
*and your presses shall burst out with new wine."*
*Proverbs 3:9-10*

## God loves and prospers the cheerful giver

*"So let each one give as he*
*purposes in his heart,*
*not grudgingly, or of necessity;*

for **God loves a cheerful giver**.
And God is able to make all
grace abound toward you,
that you, always having all
sufficiency in all things,
may **have an abundance** for every good work:
As it is written:
"He has dispersed abroad,
He has given to the poor;
His righteousness remains for ever."

Now may He who supplies seed to
the sower, and bread for food,
**supply and multiply** the seed you have sown
and **increase** the fruits of your righteousness.
while you are **enriched** in every
thing for all liberality,
which causes thanksgiving through us to God."
*2Corinthians 9:8-11*

**'Biblical Prosperity' is having
all our needs met,
with sufficient left over to minister
to the needs of others**

Biblical prosperity is not about equality of outcomes, or everyone having the same level, or even the same kind of prosperity.

Biblical prosperity is about everyone, according to their calling and level and situation, will be overflowing to others!

## WE ARE NOT PROSPERING
## UNTIL WE OVERFLOW TO OTHERS

The apostle Paul presented this concept to the Corinthians when he stated that God intended them to prosper so they would be overflowing with all sufficiency and liberality to others.

> *"for God loves a cheerful giver.*
> *And God is able to make all*
> *grace abound toward you;*
> *that you, always having*
> *all  sufficiency in all things,*
> ***may abound to every good work.*** *"*
> *2Corinthians 9:7-8*

> *"and have an abundance for every*
> *good work and act of charity"*
> *2Corinthians 9:8 Amplified Bible*

*"You will be enriched in every way*
*so that you may be generous*
*on every occasion..."*
*2Corinthians 9:11 NET*

Paul exhorted the Ephesians to work practically with their hands so they would have plenty to give to others.

*"Let him that stole steal no more:*
*but rather let him labour, working*
*with his hands what is good,*
*that he may have something to*
*give him who has need."*
*Ephesians 4:28*

*"...producing that which is good*
*with his own hands,*
*so that he will have something to*
*share with those in need."*
*Ephesians 4:28 Amplified Bible*

## WE ARE IN GOD'S PROSPERITY
## WHEN WE HAVE SOMETHING TO GIVE

## Biblical prosperity is measured by our giving not by our accumulating

Prosperity is not measured by how much money we have in the bank, or by how much we possess, or by how gifted and talented we are.

Divine prosperity is measured by how much supply we have in our faith to reach beyond ourselves to others.

Prosperity for myself, or in itself, is rooted in selfishness and idolatry; "*the love of money*".

> *"For the love of money is the root of all evil:*
> *which some have coveted after,*
> *they have erred from the faith,*
> *and pierced themselves through*
> *with many sorrows."*
> *1Timothy 6:10*

The pursuit of money and riches for themselves is a very dangerous and fleeting endeavour. This is because riches and possessions will never satisfy and in the end will bring destruction of one's soul.

> *"Will you set your eyes on that which is not?*
> *For riches certainly make themselves wings;*

*they fly away like an eagle toward heaven."*
*Proverbs 23:5*

## Biblical prosperity is a result of seeking God first

Throughout the Scriptures prosperity is presented as a result, or 'add on', to a person's pursuit of God and His righteousness.

*"But **seek first** the kingdom of*
*God, and **His righteousness**;*
*and **all these things shall be added unto you**."*
*Matthew 6:33*

*"But you, O man of God, flee these things;*
*and **follow after (pursue)***
*righteousness, godliness, faith,*
*love, patience, meekness."*
*1Timothy 6:11*

**Prosperity is not a goal we pursue**
**but a resource we use to bless others.**
**We either love money and use people,**
**or, we love people and use money!**

## There is no limit on God's prosperity

God's prosperity is not limited by circumstance, by lack, by famine...by anything!!

## IF GOD CAN GET IT THROUGH YOU, GOD WILL GET IT TO YOU!

So, whether we "*abound*" or we are in "*lack*" in the natural, God is never limited by any circumstance or situation we find ourselves in.

> *"As it is written, He that had gathered*
> *much had nothing over;*
> *and he that had gathered little had no lack."*
> *2Corinthians 8:15*

God's provision always comes by multiplication and therefore, comes to us in overflow!

The following are examples of God's overflow in supply:-

* The widow's jar of flour and jug of oil never ran out (1Kings 17:8-16)
* The Widow's jug of oil multiplied (2Kings 4:1-7)
* The bread multiplied with "*some left over*" (2Kings 4:42-44)

* The boys 5 loaves and 2 fish multiplied to feed 5000 plus 12 Baskets full left over (Matthew 14:13-21)

## God's prosperity always works through living by faith

*"The just shall live by faith."*
*Romans 1:17*

Faith is resting in the finished and complete work of Christ at the cross.

*"For in Him dwells all the fulness*
*of the Godhead bodily.*
*And you are complete in Him."*
*Colossians 2:10*

We are not looking **to** the cross hoping for our prosperity.

We are looking **back** to the cross having **already received** our prosperity by faith.

*"Blessed be the God and Father*
*of our Lord Jesus Christ,*
*who has blessed us with every spiritual blessing*
*in the heavenly places in Christ."*
*Ephesians 1:3*

LIVING IN DIVINE PROSPERITY AND SUPPLY

It is therefore 'normal' for the spiritual person to live with contentment in any situation because their confidence and trust is in God alone as their source of supply.

> *"Not that I speak in regard to need,*
> *for I have learned in whatever*
> *state I am, to be content:*
> *I know how to be abased, and*
> *I know how to abound.*
> *Everywhere and in all things I have learned*
> *both to be full and to be hungry,*
> *both to abound and to suffer need.*
> *I can do all things through Christ*
> *who strengthens me."*
> *Philippians 4:11-13*

And so, when a 'normal Christian' is prospering in their faith, whether "*abounding*" or "*suffering need*", their source and supply continues to be God!

## PROSPERITY IS LIVING BY FAITH
## ABOVE MY NEEDS IN HIS SUPPLY

## Living in God's supply

> *"And my God shall supply all your need*
> *according tomHis riches in*
> *glory by Christ Jesus."*
> *Philippians 4:19*

"According *to His riches*" means over and above in overflow!

> *"And my God will **liberally supply***
> ***(fill to the full)** your every need"*
> *Philippians 4:19 Amplified Bible*

## Needs versus *"need"*

> *"And my God shall supply all your **NEED"***

It is important to notice the apostle Paul's language; "***God will supply all your NEED***" (singular), not '**NEEDS**' (plural).

Building supply stores like Bunnings or Home Depot do not meet 'needs'.

For example, if I need 3 nails to finish a job the big stores can't help me because they only sell in bulk. I can only buy packets of 20 nails. That's supplying 'need', not specific 'needs'.

This is a great picture of God's prosperity. He only supplies in bulk, in abundance, in overflow!

Our weekly household budget may only be $500 to meet our needs and "to get by". But God wants to be our over and above "supply" so we will have, say, $750 per week so we will have an extra $250 to minister to others!

God supplies above our needs so we can live beyond our need and have some left over so we will be able to give and share with others!

## GOD WANTS TO FREE US FROM OUR 'NEEDS', TO LIVE IN GOD'S PROSPERITY BY FAITH SO WE WILL OVERFLOW TO OTHERS IN GIVING

## We are blessed to be a blessing

The "Blessing of Abraham" on our lives is we are BLESSED TO BE A BLESSING!

> *"That the blessing of Abraham*
> *might come on the Gentiles*
> *through Jesus Christ;*

*that we might receive the promise*
*of the Spirit through faith."*
*Galatians 3:14*

*"And Abraham was old, and well stricken in age:*
*and the Lord had blessed Abraham in all things."*
*Genesis 24:1*

*"...and the Lord had blessed him in everything."*
*Genesis 24:1 NET*

Therefore, the 'normal Christian' lives to be a blessing.

*"Not rendering evil for evil, or railing for railing:*
*but contrariwise blessing; knowing*
*that you are thereunto called,*
*that you should inherit a blessing."*
*1Peter 3:9*

*"...but instead bless others*
*because you were called to inherit a blessing."*
*1Peter 3:9 NET*

## 'Acquisition Living' Versus 'Provision Living'

The '**acquisition mindset**' looks forward to see if God will provide for what he has commanded and promised, so the will of God can then be done.

On the contrary, the **'provision mindset'** of faith looks back to obey what God has already commanded and promised and begins to do the will of God in anticipation of the provision.

The spiritual person with a 'provision mindset' is focused more on what God is asking them to do, rather than how and when the provision will be realised.

| ACQUISITION MINDSET | PROVISION MINDSET |
|---|---|
| * acquiring in our hands **BEFORE** we go | * going **WITH** the provision **IN** our faith not necessarily in our hands |
| * acquiring with the **5 SENSES** | **\*** possessing with our **FAITH** |
| * looking **FOR** the victory to go | * going out **IN** the victory |
| * amount of giving determined by **AMOUNT ACQUIRED** | * amount of giving determined by our **FAITH** in the **LEADING** of the Holy Spirit |

* acquisition is the **SUBSTANCE** and **EVIDENCE**
* acquisition is **LOOKING TO BELIEVE**

* acquisition looks to the **NATURAL** for **CONFIRMATION**

* **FAITH** is the **SUBSTANCE** and **EVIDENCE**
* provision is **BELIEVING NOW** as **ESTABLISHED FACT**

* provision looks to the **SPIRITUAL** for **CONFIRMATION**

## The 'normal Christian' lives by faith, not by finances and resources

The first and only question that the 'normal Christian' asks is, "*What does God want me to do?*"

And then, he moves out in the obedience of faith with or without the natural evidence of finances or resources in his possession. This is living by faith.

> "***By faith Abraham obeyed***, *when he was called out to go to the place which he would receive as an inheritance. And he went out, **not knowing where he was going**.*"
> *Hebrews 11:8*

To 'live by finances', on the other hand, asks the question, "*Do I have enough money and resources to do what God wants me to do?*" If not, "*I'll wait until God provides the finances and resources, and then I'll obey!*"

## Explicit obedience to God

To "*live by faith*" means to operate in explicit obedience to what God has said in His Word and what He is revealing through the Holy Spirit…PERIOD!

And so, Instead of stating, "I work for a living", or, I work for Woolworths", or, "I work for myself", the person of faith states, "*I am working together with God*"!

*"For we are **God's fellow workers**:*
*you are God's field, you are God's building."*
*1Corinthians 3:9*

Therefore, the 'normal Christian' believes that it is God who supplies and provides everything, even through secular occupations and natural means.

**God is not restricted on how He supplies as we** work together with Him, even in the natural and the possible!

## WE DO THE POSSIBLE
## GOD DOES THE IMPOSSIBLE!

## Chapter Ten

# WEAR YOUR FATHER'S COAT OF PROVISION

The revelation of God's provision in Christ is a common theme in the Scriptures which is presented as being "*Clothed with Christ*".

From the very beginning when Adam and Eve fell because of their sin, God sacrificed an animal and brought the skins as clothing to cover their nakedness.

> *"To Adam and to his wife the Lord*
> *God made **coats of skins**,*
> ***and clothed them.**"*
> *Genesis 3:21*

At the end of the Bible in the Book of Revelation we discover that the saints will be "*clothed in white robes*" to enter heaven.

*"After this I beheld, and, lo, a great
multitude, which no man could number,
of all nations, and kindreds, and
people, and tongues,
stood before the throne, and before the Lamb,
**clothed with white robes**..."*
*Rev 7:9*

The New Testament teaches us to **"put off"** the **"old"** and to "**put on**" the **"new";** to be **"clothed"** with the **"new nature".**

*"That you **put off** concerning the
former conversation the old man,
which is corrupt according to the deceitful lusts;
And be renewed in the spirit of your mind;
And that you **put on** the new man,
which after God is **created in
righteousness and true holiness**."*
*Ephesians 4:22-24*

*"and to **clothe yourselves**
with the **new nature**..."*
*(International Standard Version)*

The apostle Paul used the phrases "**put off**" and "**put on**" to call to mind the removal and donning of a garment; a clothing metaphor.

## The daily, habitual clothing by faith

The apostle Paul is presenting us with the concept and need to be constantly, as an every day habit, of being daily '*clothed by faith*' in Christ's provision of the "*new nature*" which is "*created in righteousness and true holiness.*"

We also see this concept of being clothed by God in the command of Jesus to His disciples at His ascension when He told them they would be "*clothed with power*" from God.

> *"And look, I am sending you*
> *what my Father promised.*
> *But stay in the city until you have been*
> ***clothed with power from on high.*** *"*
> *Luke 24:49*

The Christian life is designed by God to be lived being **'clothed'** and **'carrying'** the presence and power of the Holy Spirit.

This provision in Christ clothes us with:-

* **Power**
* **Strength**
* **Empowerment**
* **Ability**
* **Might**
* **Capacity**
* **Boldness**
* **Confidence**
* **Endowment**

*"God has not given us a spirit of fear,*
***but of power, love and a sound mind."***
*2Tim 1:7*

This is what it means to be "**clothed with the new man**".
We are clothed in:-

**RIGHTEOUSNESS**
**TRUE HOLINESS**
**POWER**
**STRENGTH**
**THE NEW LIFE IN CHRIST**

When we believe in the Lord Jesus Christ and are baptised,
we are instantly "*clothed in Christ*".

*"For in Christ Jesus you are all*
*sons of God through faith.*
*For all of you who were baptised into Christ*
***have clothed yourselves with Christ."***
*Gal 3:27 (NET)*

## Joseph boldly wore his father's coat

*"Now Israel loved Joseph more*
*than all his children,*
*because he was the son of his old age,*
*and he made him a **coat of many colours."***
*Genesis 37:3*

Joseph boldly and confidently wore the coat of his father's love, blessing and provision and his brothers were jealous of him and spoke against him.

*"And when his brothers saw*
*that their father loved him more*
*than all his brothers,*
*they hated him, and could not*
*speak peaceably unto him."*
*Genesis 37:4*

## We are to wear our heavenly father's coat

We are called to walk in this life wearing the coat of our heavenly father's love, blessing and provision in Christ!

*"Blessed be the God and Father*
*of our Lord Jesus Christ,*
*who has blessed us with every spiritual blessing*
*in the heavenly places in Christ..."*
*Ephesians 3:1*

However, the devil is always actively trying to thwart the bold and confident wearing of our heavenly father's coat.

Just as it was in the beginning with Adam and Eve, the devil convinced them that they were naked. The tragedy was that they believed the devil rather than God. They were actually clothed in the glory of God!

*"And he said, I heard Your voice in the garden,*
*and I was afraid, because I was*
*naked; and I hid myself.*
*And He said, **Who told you***
***that you were naked?***
*Genesis 3:10-11*

## The devil declares us also to be naked, God declares us to be clothed!

The devil declares us also to be naked, unrighteous, insufficient, incomplete and not enough in ourselves.

God declares us to be clothed in righteousness, sufficient, complete and abundant in Christ!

Therefore, unlike Adam and Eve, the '*normal Christian*' does not listen to the lies and accusations of the devil.

The devil is constantly promoting the narrative that we are not saved enough, loved enough, righteous enough, worthy enough, blessed enough, favoured enough, healed enough, prospered enough, empowered enough and successful enough.

However, the opposite is actually true! God has abundantly provided us with all that we need in Christ. We are "*complete in Christ*"!

> *"For in Him dwells all the fulness*
> *of the Godhead bodily.*
> *And **you are complete in Him**, who is the*
> *head of all principality and power."*
> *Colossians 2:9-10*

## How do we wear our heavenly Father's coat?

For the '*normal Christian*' the coat of our heavenly father's provision in Christ is spiritual and unseen. So, we wear our heavenly father's coat by faith in Christ Jesus.

> *"For therein is the righteousness of*
> *God revealed from faith to faith:*
> *as it is written, **the just shall live by faith**."*
> *Rom 1:17*

> *"I am crucified with Christ: nevertheless I live;*
> *yet not I, but Christ lives in me:*
> *and the life which I now live in the flesh*
> ***I live by faith in the Son of God**,*
> *who loved me, and gave himself for me."*
> *Gal 2:20*

Our faith is activated when we acknowledge all the good things that are in us in Christ Jesus!

> *"That the sharing of you faith*
> *may become effective*
> *by the acknowledging of every good thing*
> *which is in you in Christ Jesus."*
> *Philemon 6*

The Bible teaches us that such acknowledgment is always with the heart and with the mouth.

> *"That if you shall* **confess** *with*
> *your* **mouth** *the Lord Jesus,*
> *and shall* **believe** *in your* **heart** *that*
> *God has raised Him from the dead,*
> *you will be saved.*
> *For with the* **heart** *man* **believes**
> *unto righteousness;*
> *and with the mouth confession*
> *is made unto salvation."*
> *Rom 10:9-10*

## WEAR YOUR HEAVENLY FATHER'S COAT OF PROVISION IN CHRIST BY FAITH

## Chapter Eleven

# NORMAL SPIRITUALITY: HOW SHOULD WE THEN LIVE?

*"Therefore, since all these*
*things will be dissolved,*
*what manner of persons ought you to be*
*in all holy conduct and godliness."*
*2Peter 3:11*

What does 'normal spirituality' look like for the 'normal Christian'?

The spiritual person is constantly living by faith in Christ. This causes his life to flow with ease because there is no need to strive to find, or stay in, or try to keep the anointing and the presence of God: a 'non-intense spirituality'.

### THE SPIRITUAL PERSON CANNOT CLAIM WHAT HE ALREADY POSSESSES!

The normal Christian believes that God is always present within him and will never leave him or forsake him no matter what the circumstances!

> *"And be content with such things as you have:*
> *for He has said, I will never leave*
> *you, nor forsake you.*
> *So that we may boldly say,*
> *The Lord is my helper,*
> *and I will not fear what man shall do to me."*
> *Hebrews 13:5-6*

Therefore, to 'be spiritual' is totally normal for the spiritual person because he is *"born of the Spirit"*, *"filled with Spirit"*, *"led by the Spirit"* and is *"spiritually minded"*; 'naturally spiritual and spiritually natural'!

## The simplicity of faith

> *"But I fear, lest by any means, as the serpent*
> *beguiled Eve through his subtlety,*
> *so your minds should be corrupted*
> *from the simplicity that is in Christ."*
> *2Corinthians 11:3*

The word "simplicity" used here by the apostle Paul, is the Greek word "*haplotes*" (Strongs Concordance, G572), meaning "*singleness, sincerity, mental honesty and the virtue of one who is free from pretence and hypocrisy.*"

Therefore, faith is a simple and clear matter for the spiritual person. Faith is not complicated or difficult:-

### God has said it, therefore it is true, therefore I believe it, I speak it and act on it!

*"We having the same spirit of faith,*
*according as it is written, I believed,*
*and therefore have I spoken;*
*we also believe, and therefore speak."*
*2Corinthians 4:13*

## The rest of faith is God's rest

Faith in Christ for the spiritual person is not a difficulty, or a striving, or a trying to believe. Faith is the instant, absolute confidence and assurance in Christ and his promises without wavering, doubting or struggling.

*"He staggered not at the promise*
*of God through unbelief;*

*but was strong in faith, giving glory to God;*
*And being fully persuaded that,*
*what He had promised,*
*He was able also to perform."*
*Romans 4:20-21*

The result? The spiritual person enters the '*rest of faith*', which is God's rest.

*"For we who have believed do enter into rest..."*
*...For he that is entered into His rest,*
*he also has ceased from his own*
*works, as God did from His."*
*Hebrews 4:10*

Entering into God's rest is the total rest from trying to work things out in our own strength, abilities and knowledge.

## WHEN WE ENTER GOD'S REST
## HE DOES THE REST
## AND WE GET THE REST!

It is the absolute confidence to leave all things in the hands of a loving, trustworthy, just, all wise and powerful heavenly Father.

Then, the "*good works*" which God has given to us to do...

> *"For we are His workmanship,*
> *created in Christ Jesus for good works,*
> *which God prepared beforehand*
> *that we should walk in them."*
> *Ephesians 2:10*

…are done as a result of faith which is "*filled with joy and peace in believing*"!

> *"Now the God of hope fill you with*
> *all joy and peace in believing,*
> *that you may abound in hope, through*
> *the power of the Holy Spirit."*
> *Romans 15:13*

## Working with Jesus is "*easy and light*"

For the 'normal Christian', living, walking and working with Jesus is "*easy and light*"!

It is never a strain or burden to live in the Spirit. This is because faith rests in the promise and power of God, not in human wisdom and understanding.

> *"Come to Me, you who labour and are*
> *heavy laden, and I will give you rest.*

*Take My yoke upon you, and learn from
Me; for I am gentle and lowly in heart,
and you will find rest for your souls.
For My yoke is easy and My burden is light."
Matthew 11:28-30*

## Knowing the will of God

The spiritual person does not think in terms of "trying to find God's guidance and will" for a particular moment, circumstance, or event.

This is because he already knows the will of God up to the present time and lives by what the Scriptures say and what the Spirit of God reveals. If he is unsure, he simply uses a concordance to find out what the Scriptures say about the situation and does it!

*"For as many as are led by the Spirit of
God, they are the sons of God."
Romans 8:14*

## Confidence in the anticipated supply of God

Therefore, the spiritual person approaches life with confidence in the anticipated supply of revelation(s), guidance (s), direction(s) and provision(s) from the Holy Spirit as the need arises in the timing of God. The spiritual person just keeps obeying God!

> *"It is not expedient for me doubtless to glory.*
> *I will come to visions and*
> *revelations of the Lord."*
> *2Corinthians 12:1*

## Keep doing what God told you to do

If the Holy Spirit doesn't lead the spiritual person into something new in the present, he just keeps doing what God has already told him to do…continually!

> *"But you must continue in the things*
> *which you have learned and*
> *have been assured of,*
> *knowing from whom you have learned them,*
> *and that from childhood you have*
> *known the Holy Scriptures,*
> *which are able to make you wise for salvation*
> *through faith which is in Christ Jesus.*
> *All Scripture is given by inspiration of God,*
> *and is profitable for doctrine, for reproof, for*
> *correction, for instruction in righteousness,*

*that the man of God may be complete,*
*thoroughly equipped for every good work."*
*2Timothy 3:14-17*

The spiritual person simply continues to walk in the revelation, guidance and direction already given to him by God, while being open and prepared to adjust and change as soon as the Holy Spirit reveals something new to him.

## THE FIRST THING THE SPIRITUAL PERSON DOES IS THE LAST THING THE SPIRIT OF GOD TOLD HIM TO DO!

### Sanctified choices and decisions

The spiritual person believes that even his desires, choices and decisions are compatible with the will of God; 'sanctified choices'.

This is because they are coming from a heart that is constantly filled with the Scriptures and the presence of the Holy Spirit.

*"See then that you walk circumspectly,*
*not as fools, but as wise,*

*redeeming the time, because the days are evil.*
*Therefore, do not be unwise, but*
*understand what the will of the Lord is.*
*And do not be drunk with wine, in which is*
*dissipation; but be filled with the Spirit."*
*Ephesians 5:15-18*

This way of living is the result of making many and constantly wise 'sanctified choices'. These choices and decisions are consistent with what the Word of God says and what has been revealed to the '*normal Christian*' by the Holy Spirit.

*"Delight yourself in the Lord and he will*
*give you the desires of your heart.*
*Commit your way to the Lord, trust also*
*in Him and He will bring it to pass."*
*Psalm 37:4-5*

The spiritual person is constantly living in a mode and attitude of being "*spiritually minded*", or "*living according to the Spirit*" (Romans 8:5). That is, he is living out from his spirit, or "*inner being*", and is always mindful of, listening for and in tune with the promptings and leadings of the Holy Spirit.

The result is "*life and peace*"!

> "*For to be carnally minded is death;*
> *but to be spiritually minded is life and peace.*"
> *Romans 8:6*

## Even bad things turn out for good

When things go wrong, and they invariably do (even for '*normal Christians*'), the spiritual person doesn't fear, worry, become anxious or shut down. He is so confident in God that he knows God will turn it all around for good... in His time and in His way!

Therefore, the spiritual person keeps trusting and obeying God even when things don't measure up, or look contradictory in his external and physical circumstances.

> "*And we know that all things work together*
> *for good to them who love God,*
> *to them who are the called*
> *according to His purpose.*"
> *Romans 8:28*

## Following the example of our father of faith, Abraham

Like Abraham, our "*father of faith*" (Romans 4:16), the spiritual person "**by faith obeys**" the guidance and revelation given to him in the Scriptures and through the Holy Spirit's leading.

Even when obeying doesn't make sense to his human understanding, or contradicts his circumstances and is even inconvenient, the spiritual person continues to live by faith in what the Holy Spirit says and reveals…**this is 'normal Christian' spirituality!**

> "**By faith Abraham obeyed**
> *when he was called to go out to the place*
> *which he would receive as an inheritance.*
> *And he went out, not knowing*
> *where he was going.*"
> *Hebrews 11:8*

## HOW SHOULD WE THEN LIVE?

## BY FAITH IN OBEDIENCE TO WHAT GOD SAYS IN HIS WORD AND WHAT THE HOLY SPIRIT REVEALS!

# Glossary

**Advocate** = a person who puts a case on someone else's behalf

**Atonement** = the reconciliation between sinful mankind and the holy God made only possible through the atoning sacrifice of Jesus Christ

**Carnal** = having the nature of the flesh, under the control of animal appetites and the concept of depravity

**Foreknowledge** = the all-knowing, omniscient nature of God whereby He knows reality before it is real, all things and events before they happen and all people before they exist

**Glorification** = at Christ's coming, the glory of God (His honour, praise, majesty and holiness) will be realised in us. Instead of "flesh and blood" we will be transformed by the power of God into "flesh and spirit"

**Justification** = to be declared righteous by God through faith in Christ

**Natural** = governed by breath, the sensuous nature with its subjection to appetite and passion

**New Birth** = being "born again" ("born from above") by the Holy Spirit, producing the renewed, Spirit in-dwelt, Spirit empowered, Spirit filled, Spirit led, and Spirit governed person

**Predestination** = the will and plan of God to conform all to the image of Christ, His son, which was decided before time for those who would believe in Christ

**Propitiation** = the appeasement and satisfaction of the justice of God in removing the power and penalty of sin

**Prosperity** = 'Biblical prosperity' is having all your needs met with sufficient left over to minister to the needs of others

**Redemption** = the action of regaining possession of something lost in exchange for payment, or clearing a debt such as sin

**Sanctification** = associated with the word "saint" meaning holy and set apart exclusively to God and for God's special use

**Spiritual** = belonging to the divine Spirit, of God the Holy Spirit, one who is filled with and governed by the Spirit of God

# Bibliography

1.  Collins English Dictionary
2.  "Epistles to the Imprisoned Saints", Harry Greenwood
3.  Strongs Exhaustive Concordance

**I'm a new creation
I'm a brand new man
Old things are passed away
I am born again
More than a conqueror
That's who I am
I'm a new creation
I'm a brand new man**

**by David Ingles**

www.ingramcontent.com/pod-product-compliance
Lightning Source LLC
Chambersburg PA
CBHW071420090426
42737CB00011B/1522

*9780645880946*